NOT OUT FIRST BALL

NOT OUT FIRST BALL

The art of being beaten in beautiful places

Twenty-five years of
The White Hunter Cricket Club

Roger Morgan-Grenville
Richard Perkins

Not Out First Ball

ISBN 978-1-903071-66-3
This edition published in 2012 by
Bene Factum Publishing Ltd
PO Box 58122
London
SW8 5WZ
Email: inquiries@bene-factum.co.uk
www.bene-factum.co.uk

First published by Bikeshed Books in 2011
© Roger Morgan-Grenville & Richard Perkins 2011

Cover photography by Anthony Ainslie
Design & illustration Tony Hannaford at 01:11 Design
Printed in the UK by Clays Ltd.

CONTENTS

Dedications

This book is dedicated to Lucky, the Groundsman's lop-eared rabbit, who saw so much over the years, but never said a word about any of it.

It is also for every girl who has ever had to let the cricket monster into their summers, and must so often have wondered why. Particularly Caroline.

Finally, it is for the 302 men and one girl who have ignored the warnings and given their precious time to the White Hunter Cricket Club.

Foreword
David Gower OBE

Sometimes you just do things because you just have to, not necessarily because you can.

The beautifully written story of the White Hunter Cricket Club is comedy and romance in equal parts. Romance, because the book demonstrates so well how the true love that cricket seems to imbue in people gets under their skin and keeps a hold of them long, long after their sell-by date. Comedy, because these people really are bad at cricket. Very bad. The book, on the other hand, is good, bloody good, a relentlessly entertaining read and not just for cricket lovers either.

Cricket, at every level I might add, is an optimist's game, and *Not Out First Ball* is an optimistic book. For me, though I might once have scaled the higher peaks of this sport, this story is a link to its basics, a reminder that my cricket was driven by the same original hopes and ambitions. Some of us just reach higher plateaus – or might that be plateaux? - but none of us gets anywhere without a large dose of despair. Unfortunately for the likes of WHCC despair could easily have become a way of life but for that indomitable spirit and the lashings of good humour (the mainstay of this tome) which keep them ever hopeful.

Thus the joy of this story is, for instance, the thought of the Yacht Designer trundling on year after year in the sure knowledge, in the face of all the evidence to the contrary, that one day one ball will actually turn for him. Or of the Human Sieve believing, really believing, that there is a half century in him, even though this would involve him scoring 45 more runs than he had ever done in one go before.

Some of my favourite moments in the book come when this definitively peripatetic bunch decide to broaden their horizons and set off for their first overseas tour to France. This merry band of true British optimists, or true British losers, (Tree Hugger is on record as being unable to resist the pun that they always play "Toulouse") have a sad encounter with a wild boar, which comes off second best to the tour minibus, a precursor to the gallant lads of WHCC coming off second best to their opposition, their only excuse being that not many of their opponents were actually French.

A glossary of cricketing terms loosely translated into some sort of French is hilarious enough on its own. It would be hard enough explaining to a non cricket playing Englishman the concept of a " sticky dog" and one can only hazard a guess at the level of incomprehension that would be reached by a Frenchman faced with the phrase "chien adhesive"!!

Make of this book what you will. The authors, school-boyish and mischievous to a fault, have tried listing the book under various categories with Amazon, including, Tragedy (just ahead of *Othello*), Erotica (one must note the sub-title of the book, which is *The art of being beaten in beautiful places* and Toilet training Number 8 behind *'Mom, why does it hurt when I poop'*. It has also been listed as an umbrella stand (Best selling umbrella stand on the internet) and a draught excluder (still available but hurry while stocks last).

Leaving aside the obvious and endearing humour for a moment, which is all the time you will get, *Not Out First Ball* is also a reflective book, gently tapping on mainly middle-aged shoulders and reminding them what has nearly gone, in terms of talent, fitness and opportunity, and how hard we all need to work to keep the flame burning.

Above all, this is a joyful book. In a complicated world of problems and commitments, it demonstrates the importance of having that 'mental green belt', where we make time for doing something that we love. Everyone should read it!

David Gower OBE

Preface

An apology

Dear Kate

I am sorry if I was a bit short with you on the phone last Sunday when you told me about David's lawn-mowing accident.

We eventually found a ten year old to play in his place at short notice and, although we subsequently lost by nine wickets, I think the boy rather enjoyed it all. Thinking it through on my drive home that evening, I felt that I had over-reacted when you told me your husband couldn't play. It was just that so much seems to have happened to him during the season that has kept him from playing his cricket, and maybe I was a bit frustrated. However, I now realise I have quite a bit to thank you for, and apologise for, in equal measure. Above all, I am grateful that you have let him play cricket at all.

It has been personally uplifting to have his presence in the team, consistently showing his colleagues how it is some people manage to triumph over real adversity. As a family, you seem to have suffered more than your share of unforeseen changes of plan and tragedy. Like your uncle suddenly dying that Friday night and, presumably being Muslim, needing to be buried the following afternoon when we were due to play the Hammer Bottom Butsers at Lurgashall. Or that new dog you acquired that mysteriously escaped when we were fighting for our lives against The Renegades. And that Bar-Mitzvah that your goldfish had to undergo the day we set off for the Loire Valley Tour. It is rather inspiring how you seem to have come through all this stronger as a family.

But I also need to apologise, for there have been times over the last twenty-five years when your man has been badly wronged, and he might possibly have taken it out on you and the family later on. He plays, as you well know, only with the straightest of bats. He is selective in his shot making, and judges the pace of an innings to perfection. He bowls a reliable line and length, and, in the field, he is like a panther. He is encouraging to everyone and can frequently be found wrapping a fatherly arm around a disappointed team-mate. He will have told you all this many times himself, though possibly not quite as many times as he has told us. It makes it all the harder to understand, therefore, why he seems so often to have been the victim of bad luck, calumny, appalling decisions, insult, and natural disaster.

When he is clean bowled, which is surprisingly often for a man of his skill, I agree with him when he says retrospectively that it was off a no-ball, and therefore shouldn't count. When he is caught, it is surprising how frequently it turns out later on that there were three fielders behind square on the leg side. When he edges one to the keeper, it has brushed his pad, not his bat. When he drops a catch, again not a rare occurrence, we have normally found it was down to a reflection of the sun shining into his eyes from an open window at the critical moment. In short, it always seems to happen to him. I would urge you to cherish him after these disappointments. If he tells you that he has never played a rash shot in his life, then he probably hasn't. If he insists that the umpire was a myopic, vindictive twat, accept that this was probably the case. Many umpires are, indeed, myopic and vindictive twats. And umpires seem to have had it in for him personally since the dawn of time.

Finally, I just need to assure you that it will all be different from now on.

Next season, we are planning to do many fewer matches, so as to allow us more time to attend to family responsibilities. And, even if we do find we are playing the same number, I am sure most of them will be Wednesday evening beer matches and won't take up precious family weekends. And, even if we do have a few during precious family weekends, I know that this is the year he will finally take responsibility for the children, and bring them along. He frequently tells me that you are a passionate gardener and DIY fan yourself, as he is, and that it is his life's ambition to shake off the chains this sport has ensnared him in and find the true peace that can only come from a Saturday morning spent in the Eastleigh branch of Homebase.

Next season, we will go back to the drawing board and get a coach to come and help us out with our individual games; we will go to the nets early and often so as to improve our outcomes. We will turn up to each match in good time, and not three minutes after the first ball is due to be bowled. We will bat when we're told to, bowl when we're asked to, and take all catching opportunities as if routine. Our conduct will be unimpeachable, and we will be supportive of umpires whatever the decision turns out for us. We will not use foul language, or childish finger insults. In short, next season will be different.

In the meantime, I do hope that you will be able to join us for a nice cup of tea at East Meon on April 24th. It might be a little brisk out there, so wrap up well. We are planning to bring along a selection of our old score books, which should hopefully be a bit of a treat for you. It would be so nice to see you there.

With very best wishes to you and your courageous family

Roger and Richard

PS. In the end, he never did manage to get his payment for the subs to us last year. Any chance you could bring your chequebook with you on the 24th?

Chapter 1

WHY?

'My punishment is greater than I can bear'
Genesis Chapter 4, Verse 13

The club score-book never lies.
Obviously that statement is not remotely true.

In the case of the White Hunter Cricket Club, the score-book rarely stops lying. So much so, that our score-book has at least twice been nominated for the Man Booker Prize for fiction. It seems to get 'accidentally' packed up after matches and taken home by different players so that amendments can be made scientifically, clinically and, above all, in private. Pens and pencils are purchased to match the original pens and pencils used on the day, so that the changes are seamless. A couple of boundaries added here to a batsman's score, a couple of runs taken off a bowler's analysis. An unattributed catch imaginatively attributed. A marginal outcome one way becoming, well, a marginal outcome in the other direction. A polite nod in the direction of posterity. Opposition score-books have probably been purloined during tea intervals years later to make the equal and opposite changes.

Our collective memory tends to be of a quarter of a century of stellar individual and team performances, backed up by appropriate victory parades. The mundane truth is one of a mediocrity beyond human expression.

But in this case, the score-book was wholly honest.

It read: 'Grenville. Bowled Scott. 0'

Above it, it said: 'The All-Rounder. Not out. 47'

Below it, it said: 'The Charity Worker. Not out. 54'

And below that: 'Extras. 12'

Penultimately: WHCC 113 for 1

And, finally: White Hunters won by 9 wickets. After which someone had written: 'biggest ever victory in wickets.'

Then there is some rather personal graffiti inserted against the name 'Grenville' at some later stage by the disgruntled wicket keeper. It just says: 'tosser'. Then, as an afterthought, someone had drawn a large capital 'W', followed by the image of an anchor, with an arrow facing back to the name of the number 2 batsman.

Nothing strange so far, you might say. Another rainy day in Paradise. True enough. Only this time, the batsman concerned, the one so comprehensively bowled for a second ball duck, had broken off a holiday specifically to play in this game. He had driven 513 miles from Kilmelfort in Argyll to Chedworth in Gloucestershire just to produce this statistical milestone. 256.5 miles for each swish and miss executed. Five hours and ten minutes driving for each minute spent at the crease. Two gallons of lead free fuel for each drop of sweat shed. One Jammy Dodger consumed for each pace walked from the pavilion to the crease and back again. Four Jelly Babies for every bit of mockery he had to endure afterwards. It was in the same league as Sussex's Alan Wells, who having waited fifteen long years for his one England call-up, spooned his first and only ball to Sherwin Campbell at short leg, before setting off on his ten year trudge back to The Oval Pavilion. There, by the way, any similarities end.

If I'd been living somewhere around the cradle of civilisation, I would have had a one-man day of rage, and bombed something. As it was, I walked quietly round the back of the pavilion and sobbed my heart out amongst the sawdust and grass clippings..

This book, then, is for that very small group of people who not only completely understand such a journey, but who know instinctively that it should be celebrated. Indeed, they are already finding it hard to see what all the fuss is about. It is for the individual who cannot see a discarded umbrella without needing to pick it up and practise a forward defensive push with it. It is for the romantic who lies awake during cold January nights listening through an ear-piece to some dreary batting collapse in Sydney. It is for the man who smiles faintly and inexplicably during a business meeting as he recalls the one dreamy cover drive he did during the course of the previous summer. It is for the office worker whose PC is programmed to receive first-class update scores from Cricinfo at the click of a mouse throughout the season. Or for the man who can still find delight in the report of an unfinished, rain-affected match in the John Player Sunday League between Northamptonshire and Sussex in a 30 year old Wisden Almanac.

As anyone who has ever seen their own leg stump cartwheeling behind them knows only too well, grief is indeed the price you pay for love. All cricketers are lovers in some sense of the word. And like lovers, it is given to some to do it more compellingly than others. On that basis, this story is more Shrek than Don Giovanni.

As for the rest of the world, lovers or not, I'm really not sure that I can add much. Their lives are currently meaningful in some different sense of the word to mine, and they are unlikely to build on their self-knowledge by anything they find in here. A peep into a freak show, perhaps, but didn't we get over that sort of thing when the last bearded lady shuffled away from her Victorian cage? The shadow of satire squats malevolently up there in the rafters, but most people have better things to do than to drag it down into these pages. Anyway, you can rest assured that it will get down there perfectly happily on its own.

Perhaps I need to explain. The people I am writing about live in a parallel universe called the White Hunter Cricket Club. We inhabit what is in effect a half way house for addicts, where mediocrity is the addiction we battle, and personal under-achievement represents our cold turkey. But the turkey would have to be really exceptionally cold for any of us to catch it. The cranberry sauce would be about our limit, and even then it would have to be glued to the fridge. Our own breath is often the only thing we catch all year. For this is a club borne out of man's relentless determination not to be put off doing things by the mere fact of, well, not being able to do them. When the three Pakistani test cricketers were banned in January 2011 for, amongst other things, contriving no-balls, most of our own club bowlers dreamed of the day that they were good enough to contrive a no-ball. Sophocles himself would be hard put to dream up a more compelling tragedy than the end of season reviews we used to circulate. Come to think of it, he did. He called it Lacaenae, or The Big Girls. So it is a legitimate question to ask 'why'? After all, you would not be alone.

Most of us ask 'why' about sixteen times a season, normally whilst climbing back into a car at around seven in the evening, with shattered dreams lying within the Gunn and Moore 606 Big Bag, nestling with the outsized box, vulcanized bat rubbers and pencil sharpeners.

Why does nature insist that so many people who really shouldn't play the game of cricket beyond the age of six, actually do? And why on God's earth would so many of them go so far as to set up clubs of their own invention? By what genetic mismatch did The Tree-Hugger and I come together in 1986 and think that, of all the possible ways that our young lives could be used to make the world a better place, establishing an underachieving cricket team was the one? Here, then, by way of introduction, are some of the very elementary reasons why it happened in our own particular case:

1. *No one else would have us*: If you happen to love this ridiculous game, something very traumatic happens in your early twenties. You are either one of the 5% good enough to go on playing for clubs and villages, or you are one of the 95% who aren't. And, if you aren't, your future involvement in the game you love can easily be reduced, if you are not careful, to sitting in front of the

blank TV screen, eating stale Hob Nobs and wondering where free-to-view coverage of cricket went. Or pausing as you walk past a village cricket ground and thinking 'that person could be me'. Which it couldn't. For one sad, permanent and utterly boring reason. In sharp contrast to you, if you look very carefully, that person can actually play the game. And you're not a Paul Getty, rich enough to create your own new ground and then fill it with wonderful cricketers. You're not a Mick Jagger, charismatic enough to have teams arranged around you. You're not a Hugh Grant, foppishly famous enough for any team to be happy just to include you to give it a touch of stardust. And above all, you're not a real cricketer, fighting off regular invitations to turn out for decent teams. In short, you are not in demand in this small corner of the planet, and you'd better get used to it, or do something about it. Then one day you stare reflectively out of a train window, see an evening match in progress in some bucolic Downland spot that you are passing, and get hit with the solution as if with a mallet: you need to start your own club.

2. *The need for belonging*: Britain is not exactly pregnant with sports clubs outbidding each other for my participation. This probably doesn't matter, or at least wouldn't matter if I didn't frequently find myself getting into conversations about sport. Conversations about sport are what British men do if they can't think of anything useful to say, which is virtually always. So

you need to be prepared if they lead to the question: 'Who do you play for?' You need something concrete to come back with. Something suggestively impressive but utterly unverifiable. 'A roving team,' you say. 'Something like Lashings or I Zingari?' they ask. 'Yes', you reply with quiet deliberation, 'something like that'. You need to create the impression of quiet sporting excellence cloaked in a discreet veil of Anglo-Saxon modesty. Something that sets you up as an equal from that point onwards. After all, who the hell is going to check? We all just need something out there that, by the simple fact of including you, hasn't refused you. It's what Maslow called 'Belongingness' in his book *The Hierarchy of Needs*, and I'll bet he never lacked for a game. Once again, the solution is to set up your own club, with its own rules, and to run it just long enough for the mythology to overtake reality. In our case, that process took a little over a week to start, and has lasted a quarter of a century. In truth, mythology has been gaining ground ever since.

3. ***The need to leave something tangible behind***: The tragedy of the human condition is that so much of what constitutes our daily grind goes unrecorded. You are born. You do the washing up. You die. The opposite premise delivers much of the brilliance of the game of cricket. Bloody everything gets recorded for posterity. Every run you score. Every wicket you take. Every catch you take. Every catch you drop. Every wicket you don't

take. Every run that is scored off you. Every time you are out. How you are out. Who got you out. When you went in. When you came out, as it were. It is all there, writ large in one of the club scorebooks. This doesn't happen in golf, or rugby, or football, where, if you're lucky, your efforts might merit a tiny footnote in the local rag.

And, whilst no one can stop people saying what they will say about you, once you have seen the great finger in the sky, the existence of those score-books means that future generations will know lots about you. They will know that you scored 2896 runs at an average of 14.86 and scored 4 fifties, that you took 102 wickets (average not publicly available), 170 catches, captained on 123 occasions, and played 268 times in 58 locations and against 72 oppositions. Handled correctly, this can all become dynastic as well. For it is said that elderly sportsmen relive their dreams through the achievements of their children, although it would be a poor look-out for my personal cricketing dreams were I to relive them through my sons. So I console myself that posterity will limit its efforts on my behalf to 7 dog-eared score books, and an appearance of my outsized backside in a Jocelyn Galsworthy painting from August 2006.

4. *The need to participate in the ongoing metaphor of life that is cricket*: Eventually a man runs out of

new metaphors to participate in, and that's where cricket comes in. If, as Lenin once said, chess is the gymnasium of the mind, cricket would be a cross between the larder and the toilet. Preferably in that order. Each player views the current game through the prism of a different set of similes. For one, it will be a comment on the state of his marriage; for another a statement about a current relationship, probably with the woman married to the previous cricketer. A third will see it as bringing together all the elements of total war short of a medals parade. A fourth regards it as an intricate geopolitical fantasy, with all the twists and turn of a latter day Great Game. Joy is here, though not in great abundance in the White Hunters, as is hope, triumph, kindness, sorrow, misery, self delusion, grief, deceit and drama. Truly unexpected triumph visits with the same frequency as a mid-game death (i.e. once in our history), and, as with death, finds us striving to overcome stiff opposition. As I said, eventually a man runs out of new metaphors. When he does that, the men in white coats beckon. And I don't mean umpires.

5. *The availability of tiny miracles*: I once took an all-bowled hat trick. No, seriously. It was on the 11th September 1993, and it happened against a team that were cruising towards their victory target with such ease that we had already turned to the joke bowlers before half the overs were done. Tragically, as we tend to play the not-out-first-ball rule, the middle one didn't count

on the day, but a hat trick is a hat trick nonetheless. The only question at the time was whether the third ball that I had bowled had the raw kinetic energy actually to dislodge the bails once it had rolled apologetically into the bottom of the stumps. It did, and one bail wobbled tantalisingly before falling to the ground below. Tree-Hugger, who is normally our second worst bowler, has taken a hat trick, too. And we have both scored the occasional 50, although, in my case, Saddam Hussein was still roughing up the Kurds when I delivered my last one. The Yacht Designer provided the club's only example of a match double (5 wickets and a 50) one sunny evening at East Meon, before the mediocrity gremlins reclaimed him as their own the following weekend. The Human Sieve once altered an entire field setting by sumptuously cutting his first ball at Ebernoe past Point for four. Even though it was the only sumptuous thing he did in a decade, and the only boundary he scored that season, it was enough to persuade the opposition skipper that a compelling talent had arrived, and needed dealing with.

My point is this, though, that nearly every match someone does something that transcends, for one tiny moment, the expectation of disappointment that goes hand in hand with underachieving at sport. It might just be an accidental yet stunning catch, or a straight ball that clips the outside edge of a bat, or a single out-of-character shot. The 2010 season is still summed up for me by one cover drive (and I only do one a decade) that disturbed a flock of starlings on the cover boundary at Easton. Every other heave across a straight one, every ball in the groin, every expedition into the motorway of uncertainty that roars past my off stump, all these are forgotten. I only rarely employ my front foot and, when I do, I am told it has a touch of the Widdecombes about it, something like a distressed elephant trying to leave a thicket. On this occasion, it provided my tiny miracle for the season. Long past the age when most men have given up on anything other than sporting disappointment, we continue in hope. No other sport presents these miracles with the reliability of cricket, and few other teams have players sad enough to still be re-living them two and a half decades later.

6. *The need to populate beautiful cricket grounds*: We are blessed enough to have a home ground, unlike most roving teams, thanks to The Groundsman. The Groundsman's grand-father made it, and his grandson still lovingly and generously maintains it to the highest functional and pastoral standards. He is out there night and day making it better and better. He scarifies and top-dresses, mows, rolls, spikes and marks as if he has heard the last trump. He works in minute detail, with a teaspoon rather than a spade, nail scissors rather than a mower. But his work is not entirely altruistic. Indeed it is not. For if he were not able to bring regular cricketers in their cream whites, funny caps and bizarre stripes, he

would just be left with a field plain and simple. There would be no ornamentation, no point to the whole exercise. Without those hazy dots of white, he has a vacuum. And a vacuum means a problem. With cricketers, he has every chance of attracting public fame, beautiful women, vintage cars, more wildlife, and possibly even Jocelyn Galsworthy. Without cricketers, he could very soon find that people started leaving sheep on it or, worse still, horses. It could be turned over to pigs, goats, forestry, or mobile villages for travellers. These are risks that can never be underestimated, and they are being faced up and down the country every day. We must be wary. We must protect The Groundsman from them.

7. *The lack of anything better to do*: If they aren't extremely careful, ex-cricketers can turn into golfers. Like recreational drug use, this can start with something as innocent as a conversation in a pub, or even a New Year's resolution. Suddenly, and before you know it, you are openly associating with very questionable balding men in diamond-patterned Pringle sweaters, with your ego in mashie niblicks, and smothered by stories of quite unbelievable tedium. You undergo the indignity of applying for membership of an ugly brick building, surrounded by a large field inexplicably mown on three or four different settings, and attached to a car park riddled with executive cars. And, if not golf, it could be something worse: covert trips to National Trust properties, or membership of local Gardening Clubs.

Unfortunately, we live in a world where most pastimes are about as diverting as planning a trip through a controlled average speed section of a motorway, or listening to Alex Ferguson opening his mouth. You could end up as one of those tragic figures that haunt out-of-town supermarket car parks, forever resentful of what has happened to your life, and so very mindful of what might have been. Cricket is the safe option. What might have been is of no importance whatsoever. It is all down to what opportunities will present themselves again next weekend, next season, next decade. Only cricket allows you to play equally as an individual and as part of a team. You will triumph. You won't heave across a straight one. You will hold that stinging catch. You are a child of the Universe. Go placidly amidst the haste. Get real. Get a life.

8. *The uniform*: Once, in my imagination, some academic did a survey that concluded that females are routinely turned on by men in cream coloured flannels and an off-white jersey with pointless stripes round the 'V'. Furthermore, in the same survey nine out of ten women, when stating a preference, said they would rather go to bed with James Anderson than Wayne Rooney. My point is this: a man looks good in whites, where he looks idiotic and diminished in a football strip, a Fred Perry golf shirt, salopettes, a wet suit, Speedos, darts top, lycra, racing silks, running shorts, or a boxing vest. Only hunting pinks come into the same league as

cricket whites, and New Labour banned them. And, if women aren't your thing, it's really not a problem. Watch Anthony Andrews flopping about in his whites, and with his teddy, in Brideshead Revisited and you'll understand what I mean. Why, even farm animals have a spring in their step when the White Hunters take to the field.

9. ***A nod in the direction of eternity***: Anyone who watched Gary Kirsten bat will already be familiar with the notion of eternity on earth. The Charity Worker has fulfilled the same function for the White Hunters, resolutely presenting the straightest of straight bats to full tosses and inviting long hops. In the age of the information superhighway, round the clock multi-media, and relentless subliminal messaging, there is room in our lives for a game that can drift quietly on all afternoon and end in a pointless draw that still manages to delight nearly everyone. Come to think of it, I wonder if The Charity Worker ever met Gary Kirsten. It just might have worked.

And there you have it, ladies and gentlemen of the jury, the motive. Permit us now to reveal a little bit of the background.

Chapter 2

THE PRIMORDIAL MUD

*'There is always one moment in childhood when
the door opens and lets the future in'*
Graham Greene: The Power and the Glory

So there were nine reasons why we levered ourselves out of this primordial mud, and any number more why we shouldn't have. But then there is a tiny level of the underworld, according to Dante, given over to those who establish cricket teams simply so that they themselves can get a game. It is quite close to the infernal fire, and that is where you will probably find Tree-Hugger in years to come, and certainly where you'll find me. I got there by a surprisingly circuitous route.

My first memory of cricket arose, like so many of my childhood sporting memories, out of a mixture of jealousy and inadequacy. Throughout my prep school years (and the forty or so years immediately afterwards), I was the man who only ever got into representative teams when incurable chickenpox stalked the land, and the local gladiators had been forced to retire to their still competitive beds. You can find me in the 1968 School Magazine (Summer term), in the Junior Colts XI. 'Grenville. Bowled Carpenter. 0' seems to sum it up nicely. (Whatever the 53 year old Carpenter is doing now, I'll bet is doesn't include remembering that he clean bowled a small fair-haired boy on June 20th 1968, and then feeling that he needs to commit the experience to a book.)

The Headmaster, a snob of trans-galactic proportions, used to drive the titled boys to the matches in his elderly Bentley, whilst the remainder travelled in the school's Commer Minibus. Too innocent to moon at the vehicles behind, we would tell penis jokes to each other, read and swap the War Comics that we kept hidden amongst our borrowed kit, and prepare ourselves for the coming game by shouting 'Achtung! Achtung!' every time a German car went past. In consequence, we always lost and we never even got the consolation of a 'well tried' from the Headmaster, who was already too busy shoe-horning the titled boys back into the Bentley again before the last wicket fell. The titled boys always batted and bowled early on, and were therefore free to leave just before the end. That they also got to serve little glasses of sherry to visiting parents on Sunday mornings after church tells you something about the hardship in my upbringing. Years of subsequent loathing for authority was quite inevitable after all this, I suppose, but I still cannot truly understand how in God's name I ended up loving cricket so much. Deep analysis by some of the best shrinks in the land might demonstrate that it was a path strewn with many small incidents, rather than something innate in me.

It started in Bryan Adams' summer of '69, when my father got a last minute call up to the school Fathers' Match. This was a big deal as, for my part, I desperately wanted to be proud of someone who shared my ill-starred name, and, for his, he wanted to help pass some badly needed stardust in my direction. In the event, neither he nor I realised quite what was required. Fathers were traditionally instructed to lose against the First XI, and lose big. You can tell how much they were expected to lose by, by the fact of their team regularly including a man who had been reduced to just half of one leg on the beaches of Normandy. They were equipped with bats about two inches wide, and briefed to bowl long hops just outside leg stump.

My dad, who retained what little sporting talent that was left in the family vaults for his own use, took two wickets, two catches, including the ultimate sin of bagging a future peer of the realm, and then proceeded to win the match with three consecutive hefty blows for a maximum over the vegetable garden wall. Whatever else you might get away with at my prep school, inconveniencing future aristocracy, which ranked half way between arson and inappropriate affection of a colleague, was not amongst them. Among my colleagues, I got within a generation of being a hero, which was close enough to count. However, even at the age of nine I could recognize that something was wrong among the teaching staff. My father never got asked back, and I never played for a proper school team again. However, one other piece of the jigsaw fell into place for me that day. As a nonplaying spectator, I remember watching the pre-match photo being taken, and just how much I wanted to wear whites like the First XI did. Even if their blazers and cravats looked poncy in the extreme, it was better than playing your cricket in grey flannel trousers and a blue aertex shirt.

This was the era of Amiss, Underwood, D'Oliveira, Knott and Snow. It was also the era of the man who did more than anyone to put off a generation of children from playing the game of cricket, and still does, Geoffrey Boycott. The Greatest Living Yorkshireman, as he likes to be known, with all the competition that term implies. As he ground out each of his painful runs over 24 years and 151 centuries, another schoolboy would come to the conclusion that cricket probably wasn't for him. That simple fact means 48,426 people who should now be in the twilight of a successful career, aren't. Where others had the charisma to empty surrounding bars when they walked to the crease, Boycott's arrival on the ground simply filled them up again. And where most saw the duty of cricketers as being to entertain, Boycott saw his role as clinging crablike to the middle at all costs, and making a nation dream nostalgically of the Great Depression. Even the Black Death held some strange allure half way through one or other of his big test centuries. The chances of all those recycled subatomic particles, thrown out of some far galactic black hole millions of years ago, somehow reconstituting themselves as this opinionated and self-obsessed Yorkshire opening batsman were thirty five trillion trillion to one, but they did it. The result is still there for everyone to see.

And yet, and yet, it was this immodest Yorkshire bore who came down to do a one-off coaching session in the nets at my next school (Eton, since you ask, as we took our egalitarianism seriously in my family) and put the next piece of the puzzle in place. Standing behind that net, when I should have been revising The Restoration Poets, I suddenly wanted more than anything to be able to do a little bit, just any bit, of what he was doing. It was the sound of his bat, or rather the absence of sound from his bat, that impressed me. Nothing was hit higher than 4 inches off the ground, in stark contrast to my own batting, where nothing went lower than 4 feet, and normally a good deal higher than that. And, when he had done batting, he offered to bowl his little dibbly-dobblies, which he always did wearing his cap, just so that each of us could say that we had been bowled at by a test cricketer.

When I took my own place in the net, the result was preordained in the stars: 'Grenville. Bowled Boycott. 0'. It didn't matter. Something else had clicked that day. How different my life would have been, and how much more time I would have had available over the next 35 years to do worthy, profitable and interesting things, had I gone back to the boathouse and rowed that afternoon, rather than stay down at the nets to drink it all in. I owe him nothing, and everything. Geoffrey Boycott is the reason I play cricket, I have to admit it. There. It's out now.

To my family, sport was simply something that happened to other people. The limit of my parents' expectations for their offspring was that we should be able to swing a tennis racket well enough not to be a disgrace at the weekend house parties to which they rather hoped that we would be asked. We were coached on the village courts, often alongside the village cricket team going about its rustic business. To this day, the only trophy I have ever received for sporting endeavour was the 1972 Tillington Tennis Club Under 13 Mixed Doubles, during which the Postmistress' daughter and I overcame a strong challenge from two extremely short-sighted children from the neighbouring village. The fact that they were the only team we encountered, and that they spent much of the match peering backwards into the new Leylandii hedge to the South of the court, rather than forwards at us, only left its inconvenient footprints in my conscience decades later. For the remainder of my childhood, high sporting endeavour eluded me, aside from the occasional daft demonstration of stamina that was to become a trademark response to my extraordinary lack of technical skill.

Then there was that Viv Richards thing. Viv was everything I wasn't: black, assertive, compelling and utterly brilliant. Over the summer of 1976, he took England apart to the tune of about a million runs, (all right, 829 at 118.42, if you wish to be pedantic) all with his maroon cap, chewing gum and underlying swagger. England's response came from pallid batsmen who looked like bank clerks and scored plucky twenties before showing their bruises to the press after each day's play. As Marcus Berkmann wryly observed in *The Rain Men*, the thing that the summer of '76 really bequeathed to history was Jim Laker's commentary genius of 'And he's given that the kitchen sink', every time someone hit the ball to the boundary. Invariably, it was a West Indian doing the hitting, and an Englishman doing the retrieving. For me, it was the summer of Test Match Special, endless sunshine and unlimited cricket.

The only problem was that it wasn't me playing it.

In some masochistic way, there was something sublime about the way Richards destroyed England. It was a metaphor for so much more than what was then happening to English cricket: the empire, the economy, the stuffed shirts at Lords, even the endless drought of that summer. Whilst quite wanting England to do well, the dividend of watching a self-promoting ego as supreme as Tony Greig getting egg over his face more than compensated for the sight of yet another English batsman wandering pathetically back to the pavilion. No sport came close to cricket for this kind of full-length drama, as no sport does today. This, I began to think, was real life's version of Wagner's Ring Cycle, albeit without the music, lyrics, German language, legends, undertone of Naziism, Bayreuth or anything else, really.

Nine years in the army didn't help my cause either. The services either do sport incredibly well, or incredibly badly, and there are no prizes for discerning into which category I cheerfully slid. In the former, elegant blond subalterns would lethargically stroke powerful West Indian bowlers to the long-off boundary, before mingling for a beer in that temporary display of classlessness that the army always encourages before normal service gets resumed during first parade the following day. In the latter, I would get together with other members of my Reconnaissance Platoon on the concrete hard-standing outside the stores in Tidworth, and hit an old tennis ball with an even older riot-control baton.

Once, when most decent cricketers in the Brigade had been deployed to some distant part of the world in an eerie echo of the chickenpox epidemic at school, I got a proper game. For the first time in my life I was playing the sport I loved with people who really could play it, and on a pitch that was clearly designed for higher talents than mine. Initially, like Brer Rabbit, I lay low and said nothing, figuring that if I didn't bat, bowl or field anywhere near the wicket, I might well not be found out, and therefore be asked back for a second game. For a while this policy worked well. When I was offered a spell of bowling, I rubbed my shoulder apologetically, suggesting that some old sporting injury was now preventing me from doing what I would normally love to do, and declined. When the captain asked me to open – and how often is it that captains ask new players to open the batting – I said that I was more of a middle-order player, available for quick runs at the death, and refused. And it nearly worked. Fifteen minutes from stumps, we were fighting for a tedious draw, with about forty runs to make and three wickets to protect. A wicket fell, and I went in.

All I had to do, said the skipper, was 'block it out like the other bloke', and, to be fair to me, for one ball I did. Then the effects of the ritalin wore off, the red mist descended, and I went for it. Two lines of thought had co-incided in my brain with ghastly effect: the comic book notion that I could win this match on my own with a few hefty blows, and the creeping certainty that I hadn't got the faintest clue how to 'block it out' anyway. The next ball was scythed over second slip for the streakiest of fours. The following one, which was trying to be an on-drive when it started life, was clubbed behind square for another one bounce boundary. The third, the only one of the innings to visit the middle 80% of my bat, was dropped at deep square leg. I think its original intention had been to be a square cut but, outside my dreams, my bat doesn't really do square cuts. Four balls, ten runs. My partner wandered down the pitch for a yard or so to have a word with me, thought better of it, and wandered back again. After the fifth ball, it was all over. I heaved across a straight one and returned to the pavilion to a silent reception. As Phil Tufnell might have put it, I hadn't needed any help or advice from a Feng Shui expert to re-arrange my furniture: the bowler had done the job properly.

The last two wickets fell quickly, and we duly lost by 25 runs. I was never asked to play again. But, as I dropped off that night, those three shots had changed my life for ever. At roughly the same time that Gordon Brown was coming up with the humorous notion that even an evasive Stalinist sociopath could one day be British Prime Minister, I decided that, even at twenty five and deprived of all talent, I could become a cricketer.

It was towards the end of my service that I met Tree-Hugger and thought became reality. Tree-Hugger is the only man I have met who is as sad in this respect, or even sadder than I am, and I love him for it. We met whilst he was engaged in a fruitless pursuit of my sister, whilst my sister, simultaneously, was in fruitless pursuit of someone else. Communication skills clearly didn't play a key part in his strategy as, it has to be said all these years later, it still doesn't in his captaincy. He turned up one evening with a bunch of flowers, and muttered a disappointed 'Oh?' as a 26 year old bloke with short hair opened the door to him, rather than the intended love of his life. I have heard that 'Oh?' many times since in the intervening quarter century, as it is his trademark way of letting you know that you have disappointed him.

Tree-Hugger and I subsequently spent about 8 hours in a car together heading down to a barging holiday on the Canal de l'Est; 8 hours that was spent reciting great chunks of 'I'm sorry, I'll read that again', and even greater chunks of *The Wisden Almanack* (1984). It was from this journey that I began to appreciate just how many suggestive but entirely unfunny puns one man can come up with on a trip through the French countryside. If the man had been female, it would have been at this stage that I would have been beginning to wonder whether this fling could really work out long term. But it was also the point at which we first explored the 'wouldn't it be fun if...' notion of us starting a rubbish cricket team. I think we might then have been rather awed to think that the fruits of that conversation would still be alive and tentatively kicking over a quarter of a century later.

Within the White Hunter's Team Role Inventory, The Tree Hugger is it's 'Completer Finisher' and 'Monitor Evaluator', whilst I am its 'Plant' and 'Shaper'. Stripped of management speak, this means that the club has probably survived because I have known when to tell him to simultaneously get off his backside and the fence, and he has known the right time to tell me to shut up and stop offending everyone. A Venn diagram of the two of us would probably have, in the intersecting bit, a disturbing love of cricket, beer, idiotic jokes and each other's company.

Arranging the odd match turned out to be a giant piece of cake that even Mike Gatting wouldn't be able to finish. Making it fun, and making it last, was something else altogether. Early in their lives, social teams need to make various choices as to the kind of team they want to be. This is normally dictated by the limitations and attitudes of the people who set them up in the first place, and by what constitutes enjoyment for its players. Some wandering sides, for example, just fossilize the adolescent excellence their individual players once produced at school, and go on producing it decades later in extra large bright sweaters, and against teams consisting entirely of people called Giles.

Not us. All we ever aspired to was to be allowed to play friendly sides on picturesque grounds, and only ever play one Giles at a time.

Page 1 of the Build your own Cricket Club Handbook, if one were ever to be written, would set out the many pitfalls that await the unwary and kill most clubs before they see their second anniversary. (Most of them get as far as their first, purely on the basis that there is a particular kind of person who simply lives for anniversaries. Now that the

Queen Mother is dead, many of these tragic people have nothing other than cricket to fall back on.) So here are the key dangers:

1. **Club blazers**: More than anything else, club blazers. Rugby players can get away with them (and with most other things), because they tend to have the build that prevents them from looking like a cheap seaside entertainer. Cricketers cannot.

2. **Club ties**: Second only to blazers, and a pathetic accessory to sporting freemasonry. I own one cricket-related tie, which I bought when severely under the influence the year that Sussex won the double. To this day I secretly rather like what it stands for, even if, every time I wear it, people instinctively hand me their empties and ask for the bill.

3. **Golf Days**: Why, one might ask, establish a club to play one sport, only then to use it as a masquerade to play another much inferior one? The ramifications of this are
endless. Surely the best day out for a cricket club is one that, well, involves cricket.

4. **Wives' Nights**: Don't be stupid. That's what home is for. Apart from anything, most of us ended up marrying people with more sense and taste than to want to sit in a cold skittles alley on a January evening, listening to

double entendres about boxes and balls. In my experience, wives tolerate their men playing cricket on the condition that they don't bang on about it when they get home, less still ask them to a patronising end of season dinner. Flowers a couple of times a season don't go amiss, either.

5. ***A youth policy***: Youths upset everyone, and they have a nasty habit of being Surrey Trialists. Enough said. Under the unwritten White Hunter constitution, you can only bring a youth along if one of the current players bred him. This rules out the South African exchange male au pair, the young Australian tutor and the French wine importer's son.

6. ***Club caps***: OK, so we did, in the end, create a club cap. But ours was different, as it was arrived at with a sense of irony, which makes it all OK. Besides, in a spooky echo of
our future incompetence, The Land Agent ordered all 36 of them in extra-large, and an odd floppy shape that was more Oliver Twist than Alan Border.

7. ***End of season awards evenings***: The single source of poison that attracts flat-track bullies and failing club bowlers into lesser clubs, just so as to protect their averages during their long decline. Every village, and a surprising number of social sides have one. Not ours. You know who they are. Kill them. Having killed them, you

will feel rather better about the two hours of unfunny speeches that you will subsequently have to endure, one of which will be made by a minor cricketing celebrity (one test match and then dropped), and which will include a gaggingly funny story about Graham Gooch telling Michael Holding what a cricket ball looks like.

8. ***Club wife swaps***: We have played more than one club that has met its end after the violent chain of events that has sprung from one player putting his Third Man into an unorthodox position.

9. ***Mutual dislike***: You think I'm joking. As with wife swaps, we have regularly played oppositions who appear to like us, unlikely though this might be, more than they like each other. Albert Camus put it quite well in one of my O Level practice essays, and it's a shame that I threw it away afterwards. The gist of it was something existential, and that's good enough for me. Some of the teams we have played over the years seem to exist only as an à la carte menu of compelling personality disorders, whose appeal is limited to an appalled fascination in just how much more unpleasant they can become if they spend enough time working on it.

10. ***Club websites***: Normally a three-year out-of-date repository of averages, entirely unfunny in-jokes about jock-straps, or drinking too much on the Channel Islands tour, produced just because the club's tedious

wicket keeper does something in IT.

11. *Inertia*: That ghastly moment when the Vice-Presidents threaten to close down the club and no one disagrees.

Mythology has it that the White Hunters was a joint idea. Mythology, the laxative of a cricketer's memory, is wrong. Tree-Hugger got a call from The Florist, and was asked if he fancied trying to put an opposition together. Tree-Hugger called a few friends, one of which was me, and it went from there. Mythology also has it that this happy band of brothers stuck together through thick and thin over the next twenty five years. Again, not quite true. Half of that day's team never played for us again. But we did call ourselves the White Hunters from Day One, because the opposition were already called the Rhinos, and we thought it might piss them off in some endearing way. Pissing off the opposition before a match has even started should not be under-rated in the tool box of contriving victories out of a talent vacuum.

And there we were. July 12th 1986. Shaking hands with a group of people in caps, blazers and ties, just on their way back from a Golf Day, and threatening to ask a few of us to their end of season Awards Dinner. How innocent it all seemed then, and how agreeable. If only someone had kidnapped their large and unattractive earthenware rhino-cum-mascot, we might have been forced to disband after only one day and been free to continue what were promising and fulfilling lives. If only. As it was, Tree-Hugger got his own back for his subsequent apology of an innings by absent-mindedly inserting grass clippings into the small air-hole in the Rhino's bottom until it was completely full. Apparently it took weeks for them to tease out all the composting remnants.

Chapter 3

AN INTERRUPTION BY
THE TREE-HUGGER

My mother desperately wanted me to become a yachtsman. Apparently, this is an ambition shared on my behalf to this day by my team-mates.

The family had owned a clinker-built cruiser and been founder members of The Royal Lymington Yacht Club. So, to kindle my boyish enthusiasm, a moth dinghy called Zog was purchased and I was enrolled into a sailing club that used one of the adjacent Solent salt Pans. Zog was perennially last, and not just alphabetically. The water was always freezing and I seemed to be for ever getting hit on the head by a gibing boom.

Once, when I moored on one of the islands on the salt lake, I carefully tied Zog to a thistle with the inevitable consequence that Zog and my island had become two distinct geographical entities. I made a decision there and then that sailing was not for me. Cricket was different. You might still get humiliated, but at least it was whilst dry, and wearing smart trousers. I was fortunate that my school had nets down by a chalk stream, something that allowed me to treat the location as every bit as important as getting my front foot somewhere near the pitch of the ball.

Yet inspiration also had to come from heroes. One saw them on TV. Test matches were televised live and, as the 11.00 am start time approached, the excitement was intense. Curtains drawn, orange squash by my side, and sitting up in the big floral print armchair. Five days of pure bliss. I could always mow the lawn for my parents during the tea breaks. Test matches in the term time were more tricky, but I found that the Pifco radio was always tuned to the commentary, sitting there snugly in my desk with its white twisted cord ear-piece.

One Easter, my father took me down to schoolboy nets at Dean Park in Bournemouth. The local TV station was making a feature for the local news about the county team. The director thought it would be brilliant wheeze to have the schoolboys bowling at the legendary South African batsman, Barry Richards whilst the Hampshire bowlers tested their mettle on us youngsters. A huge fast bowler with wild hair called Butch White came tearing in off his full run to bowl at me. If someone had told me that he would bowl a gentle long hop I might not have dived under the netting to safety and freedom during his approach. Needless to say the footage was broadcast to a gleeful region of viewers later that evening.

The Hampshire team was captained at the time by the swashbuckling Colin Ingleby-McKenzie, who famously instructed his players that the one rule they must abide with before a big game was to be in bed before breakfast. It has to be said that he usually wasn't. The team had everything: flair, determination, charisma and flamboyance, so I started supporting it.

On an August Bank Holiday in 1965 at Bournemouth, I had the privilege of watching them chasing 136 for victory against Worcestershire, and being bowled out for 31. I recall very little, except that the umpire was appropriately called Crapp.

So it was back to the Howzat dice for a while. There aren't any dot balls in Howzat, or any allowance for players strengths and weaknesses. There is a match between England and Comic Book heroes faithfully recorded in my Slazenger green floppy score-book. England recovered from a tricky start of 20-8 off two overs, thanks to a dynamic innings from fast bowler and number 10 batsman John

Snow, before he was unluckily stumped for 498 by Dennis the Menace off the bowling of the Mekon.

I learned, therefore, like the Hampshire team to be not very good, and to be content with it.

A combination of this, and my being an incurable pedant, meant that I could still be part of the school team by way of being its scorer. Then, on the back of a fortunate 20 for the seconds, and an unseasonal attack of mumps among the First XI, I actually got a game for the main team. All I remember now was that we were bowled out for 45, of which my own contribution was a plucky 0 not out, going in at number 9 and only facing one ball. Nonetheless, we dismissed the opposition for 7, before enforcing the follow on and going on to win by an innings and 15 runs. It turned out to be an all too brief taste of glory.

With the dawning realisation that neither England's, nor Hampshire's, nor my own efforts in the 1970s and early 1980s were that brilliant, my interest in cricket waned as my interest in girls increased. It was not until my surprise meeting with a short-haired, impatient and unimpressed army officer on the doorstep of his sister's house in Winchester that it came back again.

Chapter 4

BRING ON THE RHINOS;
FEEL THE HORN

Rhinoceros: *A large thick-skinned animal of Africa and
South Asia with a horn or two horns on its nose.*
The Oxford Paperback English Dictionary

At 1.48 p.m on July 12th 1986, the White Hunter Cricket
Club wheezed into life. Someone called Pragnell bowled
the first ball at The Lawyer, on one of the College pitches
in Winchester. The Lawyer flashed circumspectly at it as
it rattled by in the corridor of uncertainty and watched
it duly thud into the safe gloves of someone called Murdoch. Not for the last time, a White Hunter had flapped
an apologetic bat at a ball that should have been drilled to

37

the point boundary. Eight minutes and nine balls later The Lawyer swished the same bat at the same ball, only to find that it was a foot closer to him than the first one, and had classically rearranged his stumps. 1-1, and the first duck, of what would one day become a veritable wildfowl reserve of them in the coming years, had been recorded. We were on our way.

It was clear from the outset that, whilst the Rhinos had all the hallmarks of an established team, we didn't. Something in the way they instinctively knew who was going to bowl when, field where, and say what. Besides the earthenware rhino that they had brought with them, they had the aching professionalism of well-schooled club players, and an optimism that seemed to suggest, even in the earliest stages of the match, that they knew and approved of how this encounter would unfold. Shouts of 'on the arm' and 'join the dots' wafted across the outfield as if in a foreign language. 'What the hell does that mean?' we asked ourselves and many years later, we ask it still.

They seemed genuinely surprised in the pub before the match that we didn't, as they did, spend every Wednesday evening through the winter in the nets at the Alf Gover Cricket School in South London. (Years later, it is hard to argue against the notion that our Club might have achieved more if its members had regarded nets as something more than a bi-annual way of catching up with friends towards the end of a long winter.) I had been paired to open the batting with The Lawyer, through the pleasing accident of then being a quite unknown quantity, and therefore potentially good. There is an arcane but elegant formula of words to use when a captain who knows nothing about you asks at the beginning of the game 'what do you do?' Your response is the key to how much you will subsequently participate in the game. Tell him you're brilliant, and you'll be seen through in seconds. Worse still, you will not be asked again. Tell him you're useless, and he will take you at your word, and leave you as far out of the game as decency permits him. So you just have to indicate, once he factors in some allowance for your non-existent modesty, that you have an occasional, but compelling, underlying competence. 'I have my moments,' you should say; 'not many of them, but enough to keep me hanging on in there'. You will subsequently be invited to bat at 5 or 6, which is perfect, and bowl one expensive over towards the end of the game, which is all you wanted in the first place.

Anyway, it was the last time in a quarter of a century that I have been able to deploy this subterfuge, and for a while it worked. I kept managing to be the non-striking batsman, leaning knowledgeably on my bat at the non-striker's end. In future years, this became the ideal position for me, in the action, but not really connected with it. It was a more active version of umpiring, really. It enabled me to do what I really enjoyed (being out in the middle) without the depressing but inevitable corollary of being sent rapidly on my way back to the pavilion. After a while, people get used to seeing someone like this, and they start figuring that he must be pretty good to have hung around this long. Some of my best innings have involved having the strike farmed away from me for protracted periods, whilst someone else scores all the runs. I am still ridiculously proud of each 'not out' that I can achieve against my name at the end of an innings. This is more difficult to achieve if you open the innings, which is why I now prefer the anonymity of a late middle order berth.

When I did eventually come to face, a few overs into the innings, spectators saw a little vignette of what would follow in the years to come. Dot. 4. 4. 4. Bowled. All my boundaries were directed, as they always have been, in an arc between square leg and mid-wicket, and my dismissal, as it would always go on to be, was the result of my eyes looking at an imaginary passing plane whilst the ball was passing serenely under my bat. Something extraordinary and life-changing always seemed to take place in my mind between the bowler releasing the ball and my playing a shot. There was nothing outstanding about the ball that had been bowled. It was simply a medium paced trundler on or about middle and off, and I decided that a defensive push was what was needed. But in the time it took the ball to travel 22 yards, I had transformed from this studious perfectionist into some dribbling half-wit, all thoughts of defence banished into the bedlam of a rock-footed heave across the line.

In answer to my plaintive cry to the Gods of Cricket: 'Why me?' They rolled their bored eyes and answered, as they would always go on to do, 'Why not?' Nevertheless, a score of 12 with a strike rate of over 200 was good enough for me and, for a time, the team.

By a gradual process of osmosis, the incompetence of the few leached into the many, and we were shortly 29-5. By this stage, the Club had been going for some 27 minutes. It had already registered more wickets lost than singles scored, and, in the sixth over of its life, it had donated a triple wicket maiden to one of the opening bowlers. Moreover, 96% of its runs had come in boundaries. The Rhino's motto of Si movet, unum ei date ('If it moves, give it one') appeared to have got under our collective skin, and seven of us were clean bowled doing stuff we really shouldn't have been doing. However, one of the features of the way we construct a team innings is that there is normally someone down the order who rescues us from total oblivion. Given that the pitch had been hired for the whole afternoon and it was in the days long before pubs opened all day, extending the innings towards respectability became an imperative for the remaining batsmen, and they set to it.

In the next eleven minutes, The Land Agent single-handedly took the score up to 68 in 14 scoring shots, all clubbed in that favoured leg side arc, before perishing for 52 in the deep. 'If only,' he must now be thinking, 'if only I had left the team then and there'. We were now at 68-6, which quickly became 103-8 after a couple more rash shots. The number nine bat, who never played for us again, I might point out, did much the same as the Land Agent, and with exactly the same result. He put on 63 with Tree-Hugger, of which the latter's share was, well, not very many, and we were all out for 168. Having been challenged to a 50 over match, our innings had occupied exactly 22.

Not for the last time, our match tea was still just a random set of ingredients in someone's fridge by the time we technically needed it.

The Rhinos' reply began purposefully, but within fifteen minutes they were 6-2. Sure, they knew how to play out a maiden, but it seemed that the Timber Matting Contractor must have slipped the umpire a fiver during the pub lunch, and was getting affirmatives to each request for an LBW. Over the years, we have tended to try to agree with opposition skippers before each match that, with only a pool of strictly amateur umpires to call on, LBWs should only be given if ram-rod straight on the back leg and plum in front of middle stump. (Tree Hugger gives them to any bowler who asks, but this is because he is kind at heart, and does not like to disappoint. It is also why he is not allowed to umpire).

As the afternoon wore on, The Rhinos came to realise what was required of them, and started compiling the runs they needed in a fashion that would not have outraged Chris Tavare. In fact, it would have delighted him. Their opening batsman, a sports journalist from the Sunday Times of all things, took an hour over his eventual 8, each one of which was a single that derived from a meticulously blocked ball failing to be stopped by mid-off. Charming and apologetic though the man was, he had a firm grip on the concept of eternity, and wasn't going to deny himself a place there by doing anything as scandalously rash as whacking a leather ball. Personally, I'd had more fun reading The Brothers Karamazov.

Decades later during the same afternoon, the Rhinos had reached 100 or so for 4, and we were losing the will to live. In real cricket, this is the time at which the inspirational captain takes charge. He makes intelligent bowling changes, and subtle alterations to the field that accommodate the particular foibles of individual batsmen. He notices the things that others miss, and takes appropriate action. He brings temptation into play by bringing up mid-on and mid-off, and encouraging the batsman to hit over the top. He is at once the deepest of deep tacticians, and the strongest of motivators. He articulates tiny strategies with each bowler, giving them confidence and ideas as he walks back to their mark with them. A good captain, at this stage, is worth at least one extra player.

Alternately, the man just flaps off into the trees like an elderly marabou stork on the Tanzanian Plains, and hopes that no one ever brings up the subject of the impending defeat again. Very quickly it was no contest: the marabou stork – in the form of The Tree Hugger – had achieved total dominance in the captaincy stakes, and his descendants live among us to this day. To be fair, he had never captained a cricket side before.

The rest of the afternoon passed in something of a blur for me, mainly because I was in denial about what was happening. In one universe, there was a game of cricket going on, and a number of worthy people were striving heroically to affect the outcome. In a parallel one, mine to be exact, all the fun bits of the match as far as I was concerned were now over, and I was just praying that the denouement might come quick enough to save my sanity. I had batted, which is what I had got out of bed for, and I wasn't suddenly going to be allowed to bowl. This made it difficult to get too caught up in the thrill of listening to two burly men shouting 'wait on!' at each other. Watching opposition batsmen meticulously going through the motions of real grown-up cricket, it also seemed to me that they had largely missed the point. By eliminating risk, they had also begun to eliminate surprise and, by extension, any theatrical tension that might have otherwise been created. That seems to be one of the main problems for me and for many: the phenomenon of the pursuit of excellence.

As it happens, the problem of the pursuit of excellence in sport is that it is largely pointless, and the White Hunters have made it a lifetime's work to avoid exposure to it. By and large, we have been successful in this, even though we have occasional scary close calls with it. At all but the highest level of sport, there is a wrong, and a right degree of competence to aspire to. Too shockingly bad, and the invitations dry up to avoid embarrassment. Too good, and they dry up because no one wants to be shown up repeatedly by an arrogant tosser called Nigel with a jutting chin. The good news is that there is a 'just right' level, where the basics of the particular sport have long ago been hardwired into some distant part of the DNA, but only re-emerge from time to time in entirely random and unpredictable bursts.

You end up knowing enough about the sport to understand it, to love it, and to want to be good at it, but everything else is left to chance. Thus, Mr Brilliant, covered in self-adminstered love bites, goes home disappointed because he holed out in the deep for a mere 86, and only clean bowled four of the opposition. Mr Standard, on the other hand, heads off delighted that he caught a skier at the third attempt and didn't get a golden duck. Here in the July sunshine, we were very much a team of Mr Standards.

A seasoned cricketer called Jones steadied The Rhinos' cause, and then proceeded to feast himself on the many loose balls that came his way. There was something in his attitude, something that we have seen many times since from other opponents, that suggested he felt he had better things to do than face joke bowling, but hell was going to freeze over before he sacrificed himself to it. There was the smallest of chances that we might have got out of jail when he was run out by his agreeable wicket keeper for 82, leaving them to get 32 with three wickets remaining. However, as is the way with the smallest of chances, they have an ugly habit of looking better at the time than they do twenty minutes later. Messrs Murdoch and Wood put on the required runs in no time at all, and with even less fuss; hands were shaken out on the parched outfield, and our embryonic club had lost its first match by three wickets.

At this stage in our history, we weren't so much a cricket club as an accidental collision of atomic matter. The outcome of the match wasn't looming as large in anyone's mind as how to kill the half-hour between defeat and when The Queen public house just down the road opened its doors. But there was no doubting that something of significance had happened to a few of us, in that a little pilot light had been re-ignited in cricketing careers we all thought were long over. For, if we had got one match together, surely we could do more. There were pitches available everywhere we looked. There were presumably other oppositions looking for scoring opportunities. Most important, there were evidently people around the area like us who might populate a club if one were provided for them.

Never mind, we thought, as the shadows lengthened on Tree-Hugger and I as we collected the flag-shaped boundary markers, and shut up the pavilion, we still remained unbeaten outside Winchester.

Chapter 5

GETTING STARTED

'Dig a well before you are thirsty'
Chinese proverb

'Don't go to the fishpond without a net'
Japanese proverb

The next thing that the White Hunters did was nothing.

We did nothing for at least a year, until the Rhinos asked if we wanted another match, this time at Broadhalfpenny Down. After which we did nothing for a further year. And precious little for the year after that. It is moments of frenetic inertia like this that give people a false impression of what is involved in establishing a club. When the honours and awards are being handed out for services to voluntary sport, it is this kind of sheer grinding work that needs to be taken into account by whichever committee of good people adjudicate these things. Tree-Hugger and I were seldom out of the pub in the cause, and it is more than possible that irreparable damage was done to various vital organs whilst plans were being laid for the Club proper.

Match number three took place at Emmanuel School in London against the same opposition, but this time with a refreshingly different result. The score-book merely records that their number three batsman scored 54 not out, but that we won. We won again a month later in Wiltshire against someone else in Match number 4, and sneaked a draw shortly afterwards. Around this time, a few of us met in the Flower Pots at Cheriton to lay down some basic principles and create a logo. The Land Agent had been there from the start, but we swiftly added The HR Manager, The Journalist, The Farmer and The Poet. The Poet didn't actually write much poetry, but he lived the suggestively Bohemian life of a man who might have, and he made occasional contributions that indicated that he was not restricting his daily intake to food and soft drink on its own. The Poet was our Bohemian, our Philosopher and our Left Bank all rolled into one.

The crest was created, although no one was quite sure why we needed one. We decided on a flying Welly Boot (Hunter) hitting a set of stumps, all highlighted in the college colours of the two Vice-Presidents, aka Tree-Hugger and me. The design was arrived at on the dart's blackboard in the public bar of The Pots. Clubs need mottos, too, and we chose Pila Prima non Dimissus (Not out first ball) which has remained the one unalterable rule of our matches. After all, a man who has negotiated with his wife, rushed his Saturday morning jobs, and driven seventy miles to somewhere three counties away, should be allowed just one yahoo when he gets there. If it connects, then he already has four or six runs to his name. If he doesn't, then he lives to fight another day. Or, more usually, another ball. Occasionally, we extend the not out to a second or third ball, if we feel particularly sorry for someone. One particular White Hunter has been out to each of the first four balls that were bowled at him, which must be some sort of a record in any level of cricket. All I can now remember was that he was called Julian, and that he attended church weekly.

Gradually, a wish-list of what we didn't want to be like surfaced, most of which was covered in Chapter 2. It was far harder to decide what we did want to be like. For one thing, we had no role models on which to base ourselves. And for another, many of the real cricketers we had ever had anything to do with had turned out to be self-regarding gits. Good at cricket, for sure, but self-regarding gits nonetheless. We knew we wanted to be different, but that wasn't a brilliant basis on its own for a manifesto. People have looked idiotic trying to be 'different' for centuries now, so we needed to start by altering the definition of difference.

In 1515, Albrecht Durer produced his iconic woodcut of The Rhinoceros. He did so having never witnessed the animal in the flesh, or even seen any more than a couple of crude sketches of it. The nearest he ever got to it is the 1562 miles between Lisbon and Nuremberg in his native Germany. It appears that he met a friend in a pub in the city, was told about it, and went back to his artists's garret to have a go at drawing it. Much the same process took place with the White Hunters. Two people who had never really come across a cricket club before, started to make their own. Unlike The Rhinoceros, ours hasn't ended up in the British Museum yet, even though there is potentially room among the Antiquities section for quite a few of our players. In fact, one of the Assyrian friezes there depicts a chariot driver with a chilling resemblance to The Charity Worker, although the high speed he is moving at in the frieze probably rules out any relationship with our opening batsman.

Slowly, a check-list of what we aspired to be, and to have, began to emerge:

1. *__A haven for the hopeless__*: This may not seem a perfect criterion for what is, after all, a sports club, but it has its points. Apart from anything, hopelessness comes in many forms, and the Club has been as adept at attracting formerly wonderful players on the slide as

it has people like me. Hopeless people are just happy to be among friends, and friends are what makes the whole experience bearable. And even hopeless people have their moments: let's not forget that four White Hunters have centuries to their names, and even some of the weaker ones have fifties. After all, true hopelessness is in the eye of the beholder. Kevin Pieterson is the man least likely to want to, or be asked to, play for the White Hunters. Think everything he's not, and you begin to get what we are. If there was a first-class cricketer designed to play White Hunter cricket, it would be the fat bloke who used to captain Pakistan, Inzamam Ul Haq. He would very quickly feel at home in the general level of fitness, and with the inability of The Breeder to run sharp singles.

2. *Agreeable grounds*: Cricket is hard enough to play in the Elysian setting of an English stately home, or a pastoral village ground. But at least if you get out second ball, and if your one over is dispatched for 17 runs, you can console yourself with the beauty of it all, which is more than can be said of some of the dire places we have turned up to on occasion. Of all sports on earth, cricket is the one for the lover of beautiful landscapes. Even the newly mown stripes on the outfield at Lords can reduce a strong man to silence when he first sees it. It may be something to do with the simplicity of the colour palette that a cricket ground affords: shades of green punctuated by fifteen white blobs, all supported by the

odd Constable flash of red and orange, depending on whether the MCC are providing the opposition. There is also something a little surreal about doing your sport to the accompanying mew of buzzards overhead, and the childhood smell of Herb Robert hitting you as you trample into the woods to retrieve the aftermath of the Tree-Hugger's ill-disguised slower ball.

Oddly enough, the strength of our performances seems to be in inverse proportion to the attractiveness of where we are playing. Put us in an idyllic Sussex village on a sunny August afternoon, and we will fall apart like the legal case for invading Iraq. Show us a dried out corporation mudpatch on the windswept seafront of Southsea, and we will be unstoppable. At home, we are simply an enigma.

3. *Agreeable oppositions*: This is more important than you might think (although it has to be said that every club must leave room in the fixture list for at least one regular opposition that its players cordially loathe).

A good opposition is easy to arrange fixtures with. They turn up more or less on time with the right number of players, lose the toss, bat first, make a challenging score which they just fail to defend despite their best efforts. They applaud good shots, irrespective of who makes them, they laugh off incompetence, smile at the most creative sledges, eat the sandwiches before the cakes and pay their match fee without having to be chased across the car park for it. Enough of them stick around at the end of the match for a beer, and they arrive back the following year with roughly the same team just a little bit older. When they breed they produce polite lads in their own image, rather than some mocking teenage psychopath intent on cutting a bruising swathe through Britain's middle-aged cricketers. They don't surreptitiously recruit your own good players behind your back, or, worse still, mock your most afflicted ones. They treasure the Human Sieve as we do, and treat at least one of my deliveries as if it was designed to spin. Finally, as good oppositions buy into the same shared mythology as the White Hunters, they can be relied on to attach some deeper significance to events on the pitch than they deserve.

The longer a Club survives, the more it accumulates new opponents. It has something to do with the credibility that just sticking around gives a team. People think, erroneously as it happens in our case, that longevity is a signpost to excellence, and that a well-established team will probably be selecting its final eleven from a starting line-up of about sixteen, rather than from nine, which is what we normally do.

We got it spectacularly wrong with one particular opposition where, in extremis, and completely incapable of recruiting a team from our normal players, we drafted in at short notice half of the Light Division cricket team. They, and we, merrily scored 235 in a 20 over evening game which we won by a country mile. We were never invited back, the only time in our history that we were accused of being too good.

4. ***A no-blame culture***: You can tell everything you need to know about a team, whether you are playing for or against them, by their reaction when someone drops a catch. Some teams fall into a stunned, hostile silence, punctuated by occasional sarcastic sotto voce comments. These, you must never play again, and it may even be appropriate to report them to Social Services. Other teams will go for the false bonhomie approach, where humourless men in tinted vari-focals shout 'Oh, bad luck, Clive' through gritted teeth across the outfield. This category is, if anything, worse than the first, as it lacks even the basic honesty of the truly unpleasant.

Only great teams handle this situation correctly. First, by being impressed and grateful that whoever it was had tried to take the catch in the first place, rather than trying to duck out of the way; secondly, by offering some witty, amusing or mildly obscene comment to get everyone back on their metaphorical feet. And thirdly, by never mentioning it again if it happens to be an important drop. Tree-Hugger sometimes jumps up and down shouting 'Oh come on!', but he would only ever do this if the team drop count had gone into double figures.

The Financial Adviser says 'Fuck' a lot if someone drops something off his own bowling, but has learned to cope admirably when it is he doing the dropping. The Human Sieve obviously drops more than most, by virtue of his role in the club and his extreme incompetence. He is currently writing a self-help handbook entitled 'Sorry, Skip, I was miles away'.

It is worth noting that The Accountant came to us as a refugee from a far more prestigious side, who had banished him in shame to long-on after dropping a sitter. He did the same for us two weeks later, and everyone just laughed.

5. *Not out first ball*: This is key, and Chapter 2 explained why. You can tell a great deal about a new opposition by the reaction of their skipper when he is first told about this strange rule. Most of our regular opponents welcome it warmly, and a number have even taken it on as a house rule of their own. Some try it out of a sense of politeness and find they can live without it afterwards. A few are overtly hostile to it – mostly for good and competitive reasons, it has to be said, and on one occasion, at Bolton Abbey in Yorkshire, we never even dared to mention it.

There is, as we have discovered more times than I care to remember, a fine line between being seen as quirky or ridiculous, and the 'not out first ball' rule is part of what helps the judgement to be made. Rather strangely, this quirky little rule has almost always worked against us and for the opposition. The latter tend to treat each ball on its merits, normally meaning they were already going to hit the leather off it anyway, and the not out first ball clause changed nothing. White Hunters, on the other hand, who don't know much about merit, blindly hit and hope on the first attempt, and pathetically attempt to recalibrate their mindset before the second. The technique works about as well as a Charity Flag Day in Aberdeen.

6. *A will to win*: None of this studied uselessness would count for a thing if you weren't actually trying to win, and trying hard. Just because you're indifferent at something doesn't mean you enjoy losing. Quite the opposite in fact, and the modest genius of the White Hunters lies in how often it has managed to overcome teams much stronger on paper than its own. It achieves this either by a combination of arcane skills handed down by word of mouth over hundreds of generations and thousands of years, or by recourse to the old adage that, if you give enough monkeys enough typewriters, you'll find a Shakespeare sonnet sooner or later. I forget which.

Rather like the piece of mindless optimism that tells you that a new, and much more expensive bat, will somehow transform your game, so it is with the team in general. Part of why we do it is the tragi-comic notion that we are getting better and better, and will one day actually pass for good. It's why Tree-Hugger heads off in April to buy a box of the most expensive balls money can buy: true craftsmen need proper tools, he thinks, and then he settles down at midwicket to watch The Breeder's opening three balls of the season sailing over his head into the adjacent wild flower meadow.

7. *Sending everyone home happy*: The greatest thing that two opposing captains can achieve is to contrive to send all 22 people back home feeling that they have had a good day. This is the opposite to many village sides where the same four people bat at 1, 2, 3, and 4, bowl 1, 2, 3, and 4, and occupy all the close fielding positions in between. In other words, the other seven people are only there to make up the numbers. Our very best matches end with a squeakily narrow victory by one wicket, when everyone who has wanted to has bowled, and everyone has batted whether they wanted to or not. The great challenge for the skippers, consistent with trying at all times to win the match, is to mutually identify when one side is running away with it, and to compensate appropriately when that happens. This, for example, is probably the right moment to take off the snarling Surrey trialist and put on his severely handicapped great uncle. As White Hunter skippers, it has to be said that we rarely find ourselves having to do the compensating.

8. *Big print fixture lists*: When we started the club,

virtually none of us wore glasses. Twenty five years on and few of us can read the score-book, let alone the fixture list. Hence our policy of increasing the font size of the latter by one level each two years, until, when it no longer fits on to one card, we will go for a Braille version. The point I am making is that teams need to recognise, even celebrate, the ageing process. They should not fight it, as to do so is pathetic and pointless. There is nothing more pitiful than a man of the past doing physical jerks before he bowls: The Yacht Designer did it once, and pulled enough hidden muscles to keep him out for the season. The Farmer's bad back has forced him, gracefully it has to be said, from keeper, to occasional batsman, to sometime umpire.

We are, as a team, no longer the svelte Gods we once were. If, as Einstein supposed, Mass = Energy waiting to happen, then the White Hunter Cricket Club consists of a vast quantity of pent-up energy, which is quite promising for the future. When one of us lumbers breathlessly towards third man boundary to retrieve a ball these days, the remainder are just grateful that he has put in the effort, and happy enough when he comes back alive. And, even when he does, the astute captain will have already positioned two extra fielders to help relay the ball back to the wicket keeper.

Where once we would all sit on the boundary's edge discussing our ambitions and our conquests, we now give blow-by-blow descriptions of the previous week's colonoscopy. By the same token, it is only to be expected that, when a bloke has made 15 or 20 hard-earned runs, he may well need a runner irrespective of visible injury. It would be a poor look out for the White Hunters if we needed visible injuries before receiving help. The Farmer tended to complain about health matters quite a lot, but normally only when he had made 50 and wished to retire, or had dropped a sitter.

9. *A Social documentary*: Those players who have had the presence of mind to hold on to every season's White Hunter Cricket Club introductory letter, will by now have built up a unique chronicle of what has been going on in the outside world. Here are some of the highlights you will have missed over the last 20 years:

1992: Maastricht Treaty. 'Following the Edinburgh Summit, another Major event is planned, this time to Mark a Franc improvement in our performances. The fund-raiser will consist of some Ruud entertainment in the skittle Allez, and we have Hurd that Mike Gatt may well Dane to appear. C.A.P in hand, as it were … tickets are in hot demand, so form ECU to avoid subsidiarity. (A small room will be set aside for Poos; and Delors of cricket will not be discussed.)'

1998: The Countryside March: The Groundsman campaigns for the right to loam.

1999: War in Kosovo. 'The fourteenth season of White Hunter cricket will bring all the delight that the sensation of bat on Balkan bring. Kosova the winter, the Vice-Presidents have not just been Slobbing or Novi sad about the lack of cricket. We have been Cleansing our Pristina white pads to make them Allbright and shiny. Hope this is aserbic enough for you.'

2000: The Oscar Ceremony

Four Wides and a No-ball
Shakespeare in Hove
You've got Bail
Forrest Stump
Batman Returns
The Remains of the Cake
Not Out in Africa

2003: Saddam Hussein is ousted. 'Cricket teas will include lemon Kurd sandwiches, Marsharab mallows, Clare shortbread, Condoleeza rice cakes and Sunni delight which you can then Shia with any visiting teams that have been Putin to bat. The Groundsman has installed comfy chairs so that cricketers can have Aziz between innings, and, instead of the old scorebook, a brand new state-of-the-art Chemical Tally. Assad note for mathematicians, by the way, as new EU regulations have banned protractors, compasses, pencils and all other weapons of Maths Instruction, which should now be left in the Bagh, Dad. That's enough Shiite jokes ...'

2004: The EU expands. The Vice-Presidents are celebrating EU expansion into Eastern Europe. However, since our club accounts are supposed to be Riga-rously controlled these days, we would appreciate membership Czechs soon, at least before the Bohemians match. Some members Gozo slowly in these matters that, not wanting to Split hairs, they may well go Hungary when tea is served, and the players are on the Graz. Anyway, you know you Lvov it.'

10. *Loving the Umpire*: Let's be serious for a minute: at this level of cricket you are the umpire as often as not. The White Hunters have only played a handful of games under professional umpires, and they're not all they get cracked up to be. After one game at St Pauls School in Hammersmith, an elderly umpire stalked me for hours, so determined was he that someone should listen to his mind-tingling stories of The Essex (Dagenham) League. For most games, the batting side provide two umpires and a scorer, which, considering there are already two batsmen out in the middle, one padded up by the score-board, one who never made it and one taking a crap in the nearby pub, means that only three people at any one time are actually enjoying themselves in the traditional way by doing nothing.

Rule One, in as many italics and capitals as you can use, is that the umpire's decision is final. Which is why each regular player has a hierarchy of desire when it comes to who he would like to see in the white coat when he himself is batting. Not Tree-Hugger, for one, who has an index finger with a cross between a Viagra overdose and acute attention deficit disorder. Not The Grenadier, who has never knowingly turned down an appeal. And definitely not any minor, who can be bullied by the sheer opposition noise level around them to give anything out, even if the ball hasn't actually been bowled yet.

No, you want The Farmer, who just stands there and looks incredulous that the question has even been asked, or The Land Agent, who giggles and shouts 'you were lucky there!' to the batsman. Or you want me. Ever since I learned the expression 'it was going down', I find that it fits any bill any time. Wherever the ball happens to be headed, I discover that it is normally 'going down'. The Yacht Designer just stands there looking inscrutable, not because he is wise, but because he hasn't got the foggiest clue where to stick his finger. Meanwhile, and not to put too fine a point on it, when the umpire tells you to go, you go, and you go quietly. Mutter 'fuck' and much, much worse to yourself in the quietness of the bushes afterwards, but walk away from the crease with whatever dignity you can muster.

Only The Human Sieve remains unconcerned, as he dreams of the day that he is anything other than clean bowled second ball, and therefore actually needs the umpire's intervention.

11. ***Loving Each Other***: Not man love. Or not necessarily man love. Just putting together eleven members of the human race who quite like being with each other. The simplest rule of a roving Cricket Club, and yet the one most often overlooked.

And that was that. One match in 1986 (lost). One match in 1987 (also lost). In 1988 we actually played 5 matches and, for the record, won 2 of them. In one of these, against a team whose name is so politically incorrect it has no legal place on these pages, the scorebook reminds posterity that, while The Aristocrat scored 102 not out, Grenville was out twice for nought. Praise the Lord for the 'not out first ball' rule, and for letting me have twice the fun I otherwise might have had. The following year we played 9 matches, once again winning 2 of them. One of these, against the Rhinos, was contrived by the old ruse of borrowing an excellent player from an opposition that has thrashed you only the previous weekend. On this occasion, the bowler in question took 5-22, for many years the Clubs' best analysis, and enabled us to defend our own routinely pathetic score of 90. That this was the bowler's own pitch, and that he was its groundsman, was a page of history that we unsurprisingly chose to leave unturned in the pub afterwards.

Chapter 6

GETTING SERIOUS

'We are what we repeatedly do.
Excellence is not an act but a habit.'
Aristotle

It seems almost incredible now to think back to those early days when we were getting up and running, and realise that there were still vast swathes of England where we remained undefeated. It has to be said that these mostly had an eerie co-incidence with places where we had never played cricket, or even visited.

A reputation for intense incompetence is not necessarily a team's best recruiting sergeant when it is trying to establish itself, so it was a fair assumption that it also needs a few other things, plus a large slice of luck. And, as intense incompetence was something that Tree-Hugger and I had postgraduate degrees in, we needed to identify these few other ingredients so as to start featuring in other Clubs' fixture cards. Given that Providence, or more specifically The Groundsman, had provided us with the most important of these in the form of a beautiful home ground, we could move on to players.

Professional teams have selectors, coaches, psychologists and captains to shape a team. They have statistics to fall back on, current form to guide them, and oppositions against which to model each side that they send out. Then they have video replays of each opposing player they will encounter, tactical analysis of their strengths and weaknesses, and groundsmen to prepare favourable pitches when they play at home. (A favourable pitch for the White Hunters would have a cash bar at one edge of the square, and a couple of hammocks at the other.) They have star players who in turn become the building block around which the rest of the team coalesces. They have young thrusters snapping at the heels of the older players, and the majestic subcontinental overseas signing to stiffen the middle order. If you follow my drift, they have choice, class and continuity.

In 25 seasons, on the other hand, the White Hunters have never had to make a selection decision. We've never had enough volunteers for a match for selection to be an issue.

Despite this, The Human Sieve insists on thinking he has been selected each time he plays, which is just as well given that the selector's eye is often the only thing he catches all season. (Long after we named him The Human Sieve, we discovered another club that had called their keeper exactly the same thing. For a while, we considered changing it to something like Colander just to be seen to be original, but eventually agreed that nothing so captured the complete absence of stopping power as that particular kitchen gadget. So it stuck.)

We regard it as the first of the day's minor victories just to arrive at a ground, somewhere near the scheduled start of play, with 11 more or less appropriately attired human beings. (If we can achieve this and actually win the toss as well, we have travelled 90% of the journey to what George Bush once unfortunately called 'Mission Accomplished'; the next 70 overs or so are just our way of politely showing the local groundsman that his work was not in vain).

Unlike in those professional teams, Tree-Hugger and I tend to be the building blocks around which the rest of the team coalesces, which is unfortunate as we're really not up to this demanding role. In the early days, we spent happy evenings in the Thomas Lord Pub in West Meon, creating entirely fictional matches in our new score-book, so as to give oppositions the notion that we weren't brand new at all. This, we felt, would produce an authenticity that would enable our coming defeats to be put down to a run of bad form, rather than terminal hopelessness. I would provide an assortment of pencils for this job, and a dog-eared set of Howzat rollers, consistent with creating the immediacy of a real, ongoing match. Tree-Hugger would provide the beer stains that tantalisingly stuck the pages together. To my certain knowledge, a Mr M Mouse is still the only player in the team to have taken 7 wickets in an innings, and his brother-in-law, Mr M Tse Tung, still averages over 100 from the one season he played for us. If only they knew. If only they existed. It has only recently begun to worry me that the landlord and his other customers might have seen an evening spent by two adult men in this fashion as a tiny bit odd.

The first of the stalwarts was The Land Agent. Some ghastly childhood trauma must have frozen his mental development at about the age of twelve, while the rest of his body went on to age more or less gracefully and do whatever it is that Land Agents go on to do. To say he is irrepressible is like saying that the Queen has staying power, or that Simon Cowell is faintly irritating. This, coupled with an annoyingly good eye, good arm and a cackle that wouldn't shame a parakeet, make him Weapon Number One in the key function of annoying the opposition. The Land Agent, who comes from, and has subsequently bred, a long line of talented sportsmen, has gently descended into the kind of incompetence that makes a man like me feel he has found a true friend. He has one shot (a heave over long-on) two possible outcomes (six, or clean bowled), one surprisingly good ball, and a nifty pair of keepers' gloves for those rare occasions we can contrive to send The Human Sieve to the wrong grid reference. Of his many endearing qualities, none shines so bright as his ability to extrude membership cheques out of people early in the season, and to gather in match fees after every game. Every team needs a Land Agent, although it remains stubbornly unclear what they actually do when they aren't playing cricket.

Hard on the heels of The Land Agent came The Farmer. Just as the former gloried in life, the latter mostly despaired of it. His idyllic cattle farm on a charitable estate in Hampshire caused him to hate idyllic farms, cattle and charities in that order. He loathed BMWs till he got one, pheasant shoots till he joined one, and public school boys until he came to realise that he was one. I suspect he loathed journalists, too, until he became a remarkably good one. Like The Land Agent, he was a frustratingly good cricketer as well, and probably scored about thirty percent of our runs in the Club's first decade and a half. The team tended to accommodate The Farmer's every requirement ('Five today, please, Skip') simply to avoid any unpleasantness on the way to defeat. As with so many White Hunters, The Farmer simply proved that, given enough time, excellence can be worked out of anyone's system. And just as The Land Agent acted as irritant-in-chief for the team, The Farmer became its laconic wit and commentator, never losing an opportunity to insert a *mot juste* when the occasion arose, and often inserting it when it didn't.

Hunched behind the stumps in those glory days before the team appeared on The Human Sieve's radar, the bearded Farmer kept up both a running commentary of the unfolding scene, and the rest of us laughing. Every team needs a Farmer on its books, if only to provide the stubble.

The Farmer originally brought along The Journalist because the latter was his tenant, and because they drank a great deal of beer together at The Flower Pots. The Journalist specialised in covering rugby union for one of the Sunday broadsheets, and property for a bewildering variety of magazines, which gave him the perfect credentials for a cricket club. Whilst his contributions on the field were generally as modest as most other players', his sense of leadership in the various watering holes afterwards knew no equal. In short, The Journalist deferred to no one in understanding how to hang one on. His defining moment came at 4.00 in the morning after the Princess of Wales had been killed in a Paris car crash, when he was discovered trying to lift a suit of armour from the staircase of the hotel we were staying in on the Kent Tour, on the basis that he had arbitrarily decided The Poet needed company in his bed to alleviate any loneliness he felt. It is a thousand small and random acts of thoughtfulness like this that have set the club apart and ensured its longevity.

And what of The Poet? Having known The Poet since I was three, it was only an iambic pentameter's worth of effort to bring him on board. He is not so easy to pigeon-hole as

The Land Agent or The Farmer, either in terms of what he actually does ('projects' are what he actually does) or the role he plays in the team. In terms of the classic Belbin model of team functions (leading, doing, thinking, socialising), The Poet works from the latter end of the spectrum back towards the former, but not until he is very pissed and it is very late. It was he, at Goudhurst in Kent, who defensively snicked a 6 over second slip from the first ball he faced, and then solemnly raised his bat to all four corners of the empty Wealden ground. It was he in Banbury, in Oxfordshire, who very publicly sniffed the long line of icing sugar on top of a chocolate cake in front of a room full of horrified late night diners. And it is The Poet, too, who apologises to each and every batsman he dismisses, as if to disown the vile competitive urges that made him bowl the ball in the first place. Every team needs a Poet among its number, although why this should be only becomes obvious when the moon starts barking.

Whilst The Poet was hard to pin down, The Accountant was about as mysterious as a drive-through McDonald's. The most mysterious thing about The Accountant was that a cricketer of his original standard should want to ply his trade in a team like ours. He batted well (and still does), bowled well (and very much still doesn't) and fielded at times almost brilliantly. Latterly, watching him bowl has become the sport's equivalent of watching Colin Montgomerie screw up yet another major. Each muscle is trained to a hair to do the right thing, but then the recessive yips in the brain simply de-construct the original genetic code half way through the run up, and a twelve ball over ensues that reads 1-0-23-0. It is almost as if an Indian betting syndicate has a standing order with him to bowl badly. The Accountant, as his trade demands, could be relied on to be at each venue on time, and to rescue the middle order time after time. He, like The Farmer, has one of the Club's only four centuries to his name, two of which happened to arrive in the same afternoon on tour in Shropshire. Latterly, in a rare example of one of our players going back up the food chain rather than further down it, he has joined an ambitious village side for much of the summer. Happily, he still comes back to his spiritual home often enough to check that we have not suddenly improved out of all recognition. He is seldom disappointed.

The Major is frequently disappointed, but mostly by himself. I know the feeling well. He is the team bell-weather, in the sense that if The Major is happy, the team is happy. His unique distinction lies in the extraordinary javelin action he adopts when he is bowling, and therefore by the fact that every ball he has bowled over the years has been technically and actually a no-ball. This curiosity makes it difficult to give him a bowl if a pedant is umpiring. His contribution to the team is also marked out by the sheer breadth of the obscene vocabulary that he picked up in his 25 years under the colours. Each and every action, good or bad, home or away, is punctuated by an oath. He swears at any occasion, never meaning it, always apologizing for it immediately afterwards, but always doing it nonetheless. This endearing trait has led to the odd misunderstanding with opponents, but also to him being adopted as something like the team mascot in recent years, so much so that we invited him to be our guest speaker one year when the well of celebrity had run dry. Given that this was one of the rare evenings when wives had actually turned up, the choice of his obscene subsequent shaggy dog story was terminally ill-judged. That was the last dinner we ever did.

The Breeder bears the burden of being not only one of the politest White Hunters, but also the one whose father has the unique distinction of taking Don Bradman's wicket twice in one day of first-class cricket. The Breeder, having himself the reactions of a beached Weddell Seal when being called for a run, needs to be watched carefully if quick singles are on the menu. When not ineffectually swishing the willow or bowling his subtle blend of line, length and long hops, he (not the father, you will understand) can be found extracting semen from livestock, and shipping it around the grateful cattle ranchers of the wider world. Presumably this makes him one of the few professional wankers in the sport today, and it might go some way to explaining how he, like The Poet, unfailingly apologises to anyone he gets out. And, just to prove that all 46 sets of chromosomes are locked tightly in place, The Breeder's son also apologises to anyone he gets out. Some may find this a disappointing trait in one who is supposed to be a snarling teenager, but I find it oddly comforting.

The HR Manager, showing what can happen to those who give 25 years loyal service to the cause, is now a serving member in the Upper House. Although the two matters were not specifically linked at his investiture, it was quite clear to all his team mates that he had been chosen from among us as a fit person within the Club to reward with a role in the Legislature. He does 'nice' rather well, and has a nagging medium pace trundle that, on its day, can get him admirable figures. Or he has a nagging medium pace trundle that, on another day, can be hit to all parts of the ground. It just depends. A life in local politics has encouraged us to give him the important role of negotiator-cum-pacifier with rattled oppositions. Being socially responsible, The HR Manager has never forgiven himself for holing out to long-on against Toulouse when we needed 4 runs to win, with one wicket remaining. Obviously, we have tried to help him forget and move on, but he keeps worrying that one day the whole episode will be captured in some book, and preserved for posterity. How can you help someone like this?

Finally, of the original 'stickers' comes The Charity Worker. The Charity Worker invented the word 'phlegmatic' and any of its possible derivatives. As an opening bat, nothing phases him. Not the teenager bowling at his throat, nor the fact that we need 9 an over from the start and he is only providing one of them. He takes it all in with a measured stare, and beams genially at the barracking coming at him from the pavilion steps. He is a man, after all, who has appeared on the Edinburgh Fringe with his compelling one-man recitation of St Mark's Gospel, so he knows a bit about how to handle a tricky crowd. To bat with The Charity Worker is to know true fear, and the bulging psychiatric wards of East Hampshire are testament to the number of career-ending run outs that he has engineered along the way. Like most other Hunters, he is happiest crouching behind the stumps, cheerfully and loudly informing his colleagues every time the batsman changes from a left hander to a right hander. Come to think of it, with all these keepers around, it seems increasingly odd that The Human Sieve has made the role his own.

Others came and went in the early years, their meteor tails only briefly intersecting with the Intra-Neptunian Transit of our progress. The Timber Tracking Man who shone so bright for so long, but who crashed and burned into tidy domesticity before any of us had a chance to shout 'wet wipes'. The All Rounder, so named more for his physique than any combinations of skills he offered; The Ancient Mariner, another predecessor of The Human Sieve, so named because we felt strangely privileged if he actually managed to stop one in three. The Brand Builder, who was so good at all forms of the game that he went off to live in Texas for ten years and sell oil, or burgers, nuclear warheads, or something. The Surveyor, who lost his virginity to a barmaid on the Somerset Tour somewhere between the bread and butter pudding and the final frame of snooker. The Photographer, whose career batting average when he hung up his Hunts County bat after four years of effort stood at 0.33. The Safari Guide, who forgot to tell us that he had played for Namibia, and who played one match, bowled two overs, and took five wickets for five runs. And the two hundred and something others who came in the spirit of polite exploration, and left again in the serene state of self-knowledge brought on by having a narrow escape. More of them later.

By the early nineties, by which time we had been going for five years, we started charging match fees and a seasonal membership. This latter, always a contentious issue in some other clubs we have played, was subject to a strict mathematical formula that simultaneously allowed us and limited us to a) contributing to our own ground, b) paying away match fees and c) buying enough kit to stop us having to borrow when we got somewhere. Nowadays, visiting sides often ask to borrow our kit, especially if they are newly formed or very occasional, in which case the request produces another fruitful opportunity to gently patronise them before battle is joined in earnest.

Oh, that kit bag! In reflective moments, it seems to me that 10 to the minus 37 seconds into the Big Bang those 13 billion years ago, all that the universe consisted of was some quark-gluon plasma and our kit bag. It has always been there, and it is all the physical evidence of our existence that there will be when the lights go out. Human footprints transit gently through the years, but our rancid kit bag lives on, with its rotting wicket keeping inner gloves, its five chipped bats, its jam-stained yellowing pads and a copy of the Sunday Times magazine from July 1998 that no one could be bothered to throw away.

Flanders and Swann once pointed out that all village ponds contain at least one 'laceless, left-hand, leather boot', and so it is that our kit bag always seems to contain a random and unpaired left-hand batting glove with the name Mason sewn into it. No one called Mason has ever played for us, so the glove's presence is confusing. It turned up one day in 1989 when no one was looking, presumably decided to make our bag its home, and has been there ever since. It presents itself to right-handed batsmen, just at the point that two quick wickets have fallen, and they are rushing to get out into the middle. It nestles among the jockstraps apparently planning malevolent things. We have even thrown it away from time to time, or placed it into some opposition club's bag to try to get rid of it. More than once, we have run it up someone's flag-pole. Then back it comes again, like a bad penny, and no one uses it again for the next five years, its presence in the bag as pointless as a life spent supporting Derbyshire. Maybe it has life, a mind of its own, and a plan. If so, that alone would make it unique within the Club. Maybe we will only reach our true nirvana when we recruit a one-armed left-hander called Mason to play for us, as directed by the sacred text. The kit bag also contains three 'Junior' boxes, presumably all discarded when their adult owners felt themselves to be sufficient dicks to move up to a more flattering size.

Financially, the trick has been to encourage as many people as possible to join the club, which means charging a reasonable sub, without making it so reasonable that it fails to get any real commitment. We try, successfully it has to be said, to ensure that there is nothing left over in the bank account at the end of each season, as surpluses, we well know, can lead inexorably to unfortunate decisions being made to have golf days and club blazers. Because we live in a financially uncertain age, we used to hedge against incompetence by having an annual fund-raising dinner designed both to give us a financial cushion for the coming year, and to get everyone together before the season. These were by nature modest affairs, normally taking place in the cold skittle alleys of rural pubs, and offering as prizes whatever remaindered cricket book we could snaffle from the SPCK bookshop in Winchester. Wives and girlfriends either came en bloc, or not at all, normally the latter.

For a handful of years, we brought along guest speakers, making it quite clear in advance that we couldn't pay them anything apart from their meal and a cab home: Godfrey Evans had such a great time with us that he died a couple of days later. The following year, we invited David Gower, who needed a certain amount of persuading, as he had heard on the grapevine about what happened to speakers at our dinners, and wasn't sure he was ready to perish this young. Visiting speakers were also presented with a club sweater for their pains. On the day that David Gower came along, it emerged that there weren't any new sweaters left to give, so the call went out for everyone covertly to bring their own one along on the evening, and the one most closely resembling new would be gifted to the great left-handed England batsman. This was one of those better-in-theory-than-in-practise ideas. In the event, Gower put the sweater on only to discover, rather publicly during his speech of genuine thanks, that a dry cleaning label was sticking into the back of his neck. A less genial man might well have taken serious offence.

For years we tried hard to get a famously well-endowed makeover presenter from the BBC to come along, until her agent accused The Farmer of stalking her and threatened to report the club to the police. We toyed with the idea of asking Carl Tyler from the BBC Southern Counties Weather Unit, but it turned out that it was only because The Farmer and I wanted to hear him say 'watch them icy roads' in public. And this was as formal as it ever got, which probably helps to explain why the club is still going 25 years later.

We outlived the SPCK Bookshop in Winchester. We outlived the career of the well-endowed presenter. And, sadly, we even outlived Godfrey Evans.

Chapter 7

UNBEATEN NORTH OF HARROGATE:
The 1990 Yorkshire Tour

*'I do not think we can hope for any better things now. We
shall stick it out to the end but we are getting weaker.'*
Captain Scott's Diary: March 29 1912

Sooner or later, every sports club needs to tour.

Swallows fly South, salmon swim upstream and White
Hunter cricketers basically go anywhere that will have
them. Which makes the decision to hold our first ever tour
in the whippet-fondling outer reaches of North Yorkshire
all the more surprising. After all, the county that gave the
world Herbert Sutcliffe, Fred Trueman, Arthur Scargill

and big attitude probably wasn't automatically going to extend the warm hand of friendship to some apparently posh, soft, southern yuppies in Golf GTIs and corduroy trousers. This was 1990, after all, when well-spoken people in Golf GTIs had a nasty habit of pitching up to your village and closing down the coal mine. We knew we would have to earn their respect. And that meant playing better cricket than they did. And being harder. And bowling faster. And throwing quicker. And drinking more. And all these things we had to do were qualified by the one abiding heavenly truth … that we were rubbish.

The mythology that had travelled North ahead of us had informed our hosts that we were City folk, brimming over with good fortune and bonuses. The reality of us being tree wholesalers, sellers of kitchen equipment, IT technicians and timber matting contractors was insufficiently gripping for either them or us, and we stuck to the mythology. This was slightly belied by the modest accommodation we booked at the Craven Arms in Appletreewick, the very village where we had organized to play our warm-up match before the big one at Bolton Abbey on the Sunday. The advertisement had said 'Yorkshire's perfect pint' and that was good enough for us.

Co-incidentally, while we were heading North up the M1 towards Yorkshire for our tour, Saddam Hussein was heading South down Highway Number 6 on his way to Basra and Kuwait beyond. Tellingly, Elton John's *Sacrifice* was riding high in the charts that weekend, and *Clear and Present Danger* was doing it for Tom Clancey in the book shops. In the Tetleys North Yorkshire Village League, Bolton Abbey were a notch off the top, a fact that, before the age of availability of instant research on the world wide web, had significantly eluded us when we were setting the tour up. If we couldn't beat a pub side in the tiny village of Cheriton, among the Hampshire chalk streams, there was just that infinitesimal possibility that we might not beat the kind of team that ended up doing Lords finals. But as yet, we knew nothing.

One of the features of the White Hunters is how many of our 302 or so players over the years have turned up, taken a look, and never played for us again. The early score-books are full of names like Gilbert, Farrer, Winsloe and – even – Hunter, who shone briefly and then burned out on the horizon. A Gauss distribution curve listing all appearances by individuals, by number, would break the standard rule and look less like the classic bell-shape, and more like a side-on armchair, or a feeding squirrel. The Yorkshire tour had one of these, a son of the High Veldt called Richard, who everyone liked, but who presumably preferred his cricket slightly spicier than we could provide. It probably didn't help that he bowled only one over all weekend and didn't get to bat in either match. However, he did bring along his own bespoke, folding recliner seat, and was thus appointed the club's solitary chairman in perpetuity.

The Saturday match at Appletreewick was arresting in two

distinct ways: Appletreewick neither really had a cricket team, nor a cricket pitch. Strangely, the village name was pronounced without the 'ple' or the 'ree' bits. What they did have was an agreeable enough field which the obliging farmer was planning on harvesting with a tractor the following week, and presumably preparing a square with a scythe. My local contact, as the following day would prove, clearly liked to get both sublime and ridiculous into the same weekend whenever he could. This all made for interesting cricket. As soon as the ball left the square it was completely invisible, with the result that a batsman was more likely to get three or four runs by nurdling it into the nearby vegetation than attempting to heave it into the adjoining River Wharf. The score-book records the hosts as winning the toss and batting. The score-book also records that their innings lasted only from 2.45pm (Hurst and Pitchers arrive at the wicket) till 3.46pm (Mason bowled HR Manager for 0), during which time we managed to put down 15.5 overs, which wasn't bad going. The pick of the bowlers, seven of whom took wickets, was rather unusually The Tree-Hugger with the analysis of 2-8 off 2 overs. Appletreewick had made 68 all out and Yorkshire cricket, at this point anyway, held few terrors for us.

It held even fewer when The Timber Matting Contractor dumped three of his first four balls received into the road, an adjacent allotment and the Wharf respectively, before subtly pushing the fifth into a patch of nettles a few feet away and getting an all-run four. The score rocketed upwards like a surprised pheasant to 37-0 off 3 overs, and the image of a close-fought encounter reaching its denouement just before the pubs opened again that evening receded into the Yorkshire air. We retired him and then went through one of those leitmotif experiences that have always seemed to define our progress, a triple wicket maiden that reduced us to 37-3 off 4. That I was the middle one of the near hat-trick came as no surprise to me, to my team mates or to Mr Spratt who bowled the over; somehow it was always going to happen. Normal service was swiftly resumed, and the match was as good as won by two consecutive sixes into the allotments by the IT Technician. It was 4.15, and tea hadn't even arrived yet, let alone beer. In the land of the blind, however, the one-eyed man is king, and a victory is a victory. In celebration, we lay on the knee length grass of the square quietly savouring it, and gently dropping off to sleep.

Rarely ones to let reality get in the way of a passing stereotype, we slowly worked out that flat hats, racing pigeons, coal in bath tubs and black pudding were all conspicuous by their absence. Moreover, there wasn't a whippet in sight, and the tightest wallet in the county belonged not to someone called Hardcastle or Higginbottom, but firmly in the back pocket of The Sponge, one of our guest players. Almost disappointingly, Yorkshire consisted of lots of genuinely kind people who simply wanted us to have a good time. And, as we smacked our lips on the final pint of the Saturday evening, eleven of them were turning in a few miles away to get a good night's rest before the exertions of tomorrow's match.

Never let it be said that we lack ambition. OK, we lack ambition. But we do understand how to work our way towards a significant event, something into which category the match against Bolton Abbey was fast developing. At breakfast, The Land Agent asked the waitress what we might expect in terms of competition that afternoon, and after a few minutes, she re-appeared with her boss.

'You any good?' he asked.

The Land Agent indicated that we weren't.

'You'll bloody need to be,' he went on. 'You got insurance?'

The Land Agent didn't think so.

'Get some,' he said. 'That way you can get ambulance to take you all t'way back down South'.

This didn't look good, and The Timber Matting Contractor quietly choked on his Sultana Bran.

A few hours later, we were preparing for the match in the time honoured way by drinking too much at The Devonshire Arms, a large, and ruinously expensive, country house hotel just opposite the ground. A family of wounded buffalos would have had difficulty in charging more energetically than the staff did here, and the opposition was unsurprisingly drinking elsewhere. Also, as we passed the ground, we noticed two slightly worrying developments: the ground was surrounded by sponsors' advertising hoardings, and there were two professional umpires setting up the stumps. At this early point in the Club's life, we had never met a professional umpire, and certainly never been sponsored. To make things worse, three big lads in sawn-off tee-shirts, lads who were clearly part of the team, were bowling what looked distinctly like improvised explosive devices at each other in the nets. We weren't a confident lot at the best of times, but we were just getting the first inkling of the supreme stupidity of our decision to enter into a match of this seriousness. It was up there with Tony Greig's decision to bounce Dennis Lillee in the 1975 Ashes, or Fred Goodwin telling the RBS Board, 'Hey, I've got a great idea. Let's buy an expensive Dutch Bank.'

In sharp contrast to us, hardened Yorkshire cricketers don't do limited overs games unless its a knock-out in the League. That's for pussies. They do declaration games, instead. This, they find, allows plenty of opportunity to perform gritty, monosyllabic deeds in the Heathcliffe mould, and moreover, it avoids any risk of the game threatening to break out into something enjoyable. It works like this. One team bats boringly and responsibly until it decides not to any more, when it declares the innings closed and the other team bats tediously and remorselessly until just before the pub opens.

At which point the umpire shouts 'Twenty overs, lads', and someone called Seth presents a dead bat to 100 out of the next 120 balls, and it all comes to a merciful end as a charmless draw. Someone says 'Aye, that were good', and everyone troops off for a bath. With hedonistic pleasure-seekers like this around, even we were smart enough to work out that our 'not out first ball' ploy would go down about as well as an errant sausage in the synagogue fridge, were we to request it. For the only time in our history, we never even had the courage to mention it.

There's something infinitely satisfying about a cricket match that hasn't begun. By definition, of course, something that hasn't begun can't yet have gone wrong. That is certainly the way we look at it. Dreams are still hard currency at this point, and everything is pristine. To look out on a newly-prepared wicket is to glimpse a magic world through the wardrobe, a world of achievement to come and disappointments to be routed. The moment you walk out for the toss represents the last instant that you, as captain, have not been seen through for the fraud you are. The opposition know only that you are the skipper, and will have formed the not unreasonable opinion that this post must have been achieved by merit. You are believable because you are in the right kit, have a team at your disposal and, most importantly, you are using the right jargon. From that point on, it is routinely downhill. Before the match, a ground is an Elysian field filling up with a cast of epic Greek heroes. Afterwards, it is a nightmare post-battle scene, where the wounded survivors are being bayoneted by deserters from their own side.

Bolton Abbey's cheerful skipper came to fetch me simultaneously out of this reverie and the pub for the toss, with the news that 'it were playin' a bit lively'. Brilliant, just brilliant. All this worry and now even the pitch was playing up. Things went from bad to worse when I called correctly. The team policy is that in the unfortunate event of winning the toss, you put the much stronger side in. At least that way, they will stay in for at least half the match, and it is likely that the game will go on as far as tea. Against all proper Yorkshire logic, and after enough indecision to earn me five years free membership of the Liberal Democrats, I told him we would field. He stared at me and asked if I was sure. I tried to look calculating and said, yes, I was sure. He shrugged and shook hands. My decision did not pass unappreciated when it was relayed by the skipper to the Bolton Abbey team, where gales of ill-suppressed laughter rang out of the home changing room. ''E bloody what?!' someone asked.

Geoffrey Boycott's grandmother could have batted with a stick of rhubarb against what we served up in the name of bowling, if only he and she had been there. The ghastly thought suddenly dawned on the more geeky of us that GB might even have played here himself once.

The openers struggled their way to 123-0 in a handful of

overs, before recognising this for what it was (a drawn-out beer match) and flinging the bat along with the rest of their team to 280-7. The conclusion to their innings came when Tree-Hugger came on. Having bowled a long hop that got hit into the pub car park via the aerial route, Bolton Abbey suddenly announced that 'that were it', and declared the innings closed one ball into his over. The All-Rounder voiced a suspicion that this had something to do with the bowler's characteristic of sticking his tongue half way down his chin during the delivery stride. It was just too much for them.

There is also something infinitely satisfying about the half way point in a match. By definition, of course, something that hasn't been completed can't yet have been lost. Some small part of the opposition consciousness must, should, could, just conceivably might, be wondering whether they have declared too early and have given the game away. And whilst the sun beat fiercely down on the pitch, The HR Manager came back from the toilets behind the pavilion with the encouraging news that a huge black cloud had parked itself over the nearby Pennines, and was making encouraging glances in the direction of the ground. There was little or no wind, but the optimists among us started to believe that this match could be saved by the weather. In celebration of this, Tree-Hugger and The All-Rounder were sent in to open.

Batting is a funny old thing. A bowler can have a bad ball,

a bad over, even a bad half-hour, and yet still end up having a good game. A batsman, on the other hand, is always one nervy twitch away from extinction. Professor Read Montague famously conducted a study in which he demonstrated that, faced with a blind tasting between Coke and Pepsi, the majority preferred Pepsi, whereas when they were shown the two branded cans, almost everyone went for the red one. In the first case, he pointed out, the brain's conscious side was busy (meaning people really did prefer Pepsi), whereas in the second, it was the pre-frontal cortex at work (meaning that Coke's marketing efforts had buried themselves deep in the subconscious, and people no longer thought about it). He would have found the same thing with White Hunter batsmen, only substituting slow and quick bowlers for Coke and Pepsi. We all shake in our boots at the sight of a young bowler spraying it around at 80 mph, when in reality he is extraordinarily easy to score off. Whilst, at the other end of the scale, we all lick our lips speculatively when a slow trundler comes on, even going so far as to beg the skipper to change the batting order in our favour. Poor fools. That slow trundler has your demise written all over his face, and he will have you gone within three balls. He has spent a lifetime discovering this, and has become slower, and more effective, every passing season. Conscious. Subconscious. And then the slow dawning of realisation that it doesn't matter any more as you're useless anyway.

However, Geoffrey Boycott's grandmother would have

had as much trouble as we did in coping with the missiles Messrs Cawley and Tiffany served up to us in the next 14 overs. A suit of armour would have come in handy; so would a riot shield plus one of those old-fashioned diving suits that Captain Haddock wore when he was not doing something inappropriate with Tintin. It was the first time in our history that we had come across two quick and accurate bowlers and, to be honest, we didn't really know what to do with them.

Cawley's run-up started somewhere in East Lancashire, before winding over the Pennines, and then using the downhill slope past Skipton to get some real speed up, before releasing the ball from the west once in the Parish of Bolton Abbey. The All-Rounder somehow saw out a maiden, although five of the six balls went nowhere near his bat. Tiffany started his own run-up on the coast in Bridlington, and ran due west through Harrogate, before delivering his ball from the East side of the ground. The keeper positioned himself somewhere up on the grouse moors above Bolton Abbey for both of them. Tree-Hugger missed everything in the second over until the 6th ball took an edge, and flew over second slip to third man for a single. 1-0 in 2 overs, and not looking good. Cawley bowled out another maiden to The All-Rounder. 1-0 in 3 overs. Tree-Hugger was bowled during the next wicket maiden by Tiffany, leaving the makings of a timber yard in his wake as he headed off to the pavilion. 1-1 in 4 overs. Computer predictions at this stage suggested that we would be 10 all out after 40 overs. However, the big black cloud had wandered a few yards closer to the ground. There was no doubt that it was expressing an interest in what we were up to.

Things went a bit better for a spell, as The Brand Builder and The Farmer tucked into the change bowlers. After 22 overs or so, we were 85-2, and just beginning to wonder if we could accelerate and win. Temporary success has the habit of giving us ambitions beyond our station, and we are generally brought down to earth with a thump. Then we were 85-3, then 86-4, then 87-5 and then 90-6. Most of the problem came from the fact that Tiffany's brother, who had been a bit poorly with hay fever earlier on in the afternoon, revealed himself as the real bowler in the family once the anti-histamine had kicked in. He started taking wickets with almost obscene abandon. 102-7 when The Land Agent drilled one back to the bowler. 103-8 when The HR Manager tried to do roughly the same thing, only didn't hit the ball before it hit his stumps. The big black cloud appeared to have noticed what was going on, and was hanging around on the Western edge of the ground, as if waiting to be invited in. Given that we had at least 20 overs to survive before we could claim a draw, we duly issued the invitation, and another one to any members of its extended family it wanted to bring along. The IT Consultant and I were now what stood between the White Hunters and oblivion. If you ever find yourself facing oblivion, I would venture to suggest that you would want something a bit more substantial than me and a cloud in between.

Part of the psychology of under-achievement in which I have a postgraduate doctorate can be best described by the question: 'why does it always happen to me?' This is normal practise for sportsmen of a certain standard. I sit on the boundary's edge for hours on end watching one of my equally sub-standard colleagues getting fed delicious long hops a foot either side of the wicket, and I think to myself: 'why couldn't it be me?' I watch his score mount: 15, 25, 40, 50, and I utter the old, old prayer: 'Please God: keep this bowler on for when I come in'. But then the batsman retires, and I go in. Mysteriously, the opening bowler, having replenished his aggression on a diet of raw meat in the interlude, comes back into the attack. He is furious, and there is no one in the world he dislikes more than me. I last three balls, the first two of which I miss, before carving a straight one into the safe hands of a delighted mid-off. It has suddenly become a different game before, equally suddenly, going back to what it was before I came in. All I have ever wanted out of life is the occasional short-pitched ball, about a foot outside the off stump, which I can club to the point boundary to tumultuous applause. Or a severely disoriented person being asked to bowl one over just after I have come to the wicket. Or someone visually handicapped to face an over from me. Or someone with a fatal allergy to leather to be underneath a catch offered by me. It's not a lot to ask, really, but it certainly wasn't about to be offered at Bolton Abbey.

The next four or five overs passed in something of a blur. The presence of the cloud had tapped the Bolton Abbey captain on the shoulder, as well as us, and it had spurred him into putting the Tiffany brothers on in harness, in one final effort to take the last couple of wickets before the rain fell. If I had known how to play a forward defensive, I would have done it. Equally, if I had understood how to offer a back foot defensive, I might have tried that as well. My signature shot, the 9 iron heave over deep mid-wicket, was about as much use as a self-esteem course to Mark Nicholas, as everything was speared in at my toes. As it was, I lunged forward at each ball in some horrible parody of Victorian insanity, and managed to stay there. Sometimes I hit the ball. Other times it hit me. Occasionally, we hit each other. Once I caught an inside edge, and the ball raced past the leg stump on its way to the fine leg boundary. Choice stage whispers were offered by the keeper back to the bowler, and the unkindest thing was that I couldn't argue against the truth of any of them. The gist was that a better batsman than me would be rather nearer the ball than I was, and might consequently be offering the odd edge. When the deluge came, we had put on 7 runs in 9 overs, and we ran back to the shelter of the pavilion as self-appointed heroes.

By the time the rain eased up, the wicket was under two inches of water, and further play was quite impossible. Tree-Hugger, whose career in amateur dramatics has been marginally more successful than his cricketing one, made lots of appropriately regretful noises before we all headed back to the visitors' changing room for a team hug. After all, a draw is a draw, and a tour of Yorkshire without a defeat is, well, far more than we deserved. Whilst there was slightly muted enthusiasm from Bolton Abbey to the idea of a return tour, the day had been a good one for everyone, and they had measured up in every respect bar one to our notion of what a good opposition side should be: hospitable, cheerful and competitive. If only they could have been a little worse at cricket.

Chapter 8

CAPTAIN MY CAPTAIN

'That in the captain's but a choleric word,
Which in the soldier is flat blasphemy
'Shakespeare: Measure for Measure

Deep in the dim shadows where mythology and history converge, the White Hunters went from being a loose group of occasional cricketers to something that bore a vague resemblance to an actual cricket team.

Our first fixture card (as opposed to the tatty old bit of A4 paper which had preceded it) followed the Yorkshire Tour. We had a hard core of people, at least 50% of whom could be relied upon to pitch up to most matches. We had our own pitch. We even had our own pub, even though at times it seemed that it was them doing us the favour rather than vice-versa. All we needed now was a bit of leadership.

Captaincy, the overworked concept without which no cricket book seems complete, is a dark art down our way. It fascinates us, diverts us for hours, and we all like to give it a go at some stage in the season. However, the God who had delivered us from evil at Bolton Abbey, had other ideas when it came to giving the club the guidance that it needed, both on and off the pitch, in its early days. By tradition, Tree-Hugger and I would captain alternate matches and then compare notes at the end of the season, so as to see if any patterns emerged. As it happened, they did. The pattern that emerged was that neither of us really won much, so the differentiation had to happen through the manner of losing. Fundamentally, it always seemed to come down to a question of leadership. And leadership needed to start with just a little bit of research.

Kurt Lewin's 1939 model of leadership styles (authoritarian; democratic; laissez-faire) was where we might have kicked off, had we known better. Tree-Hugger, we analysed, would tend to start all his matches virtually off the authoritarian scale, barking out orders and getting cross and frustrated with people. Then he would work his way gently eastwards on the grid until he ended up pathetically appealing to the players' better natures, normally a pointless and bad mistake. I, on the other hand, started each game in cringingly democratic style until circumstance, added to my background as a regular soldier, shunted me into the realms of foaming-mouthed dictatorship during the closing overs. This made for interesting psychological profiling, but not many victories. There had to be another way, and there was.

We bought a remaindered copy of Gary Yukl's classic textbook Leadership in Organisations, threw it away and started to get down to the meaty business of cricket.

Before we did that, we needed to consider how to get the best out of a habitually under-performing team, and our search led us to Bruce Tuckman. Mr Tuckman came out with his four phases of corporate team development theory in 1965, and I like to think he had people like us in mind when he did so. Forming, storming, norming and reforming. With me so far? I think the whole process is supposed to take an organization about 2 months, which is a shame as we are only two phases in after a quarter of a century. However, Tree-Hugger and I took our responsibilities seriously, and another stupefyingly dull text book was acquired in the interests of excellence.

In the forming phase, we discovered, the leaders are looked to incessantly for guidance on team aims, objectives and external relationships, and there is a high dependence on the leadership, and 'little agreement on team aims'. We liked the bit about dependence, and agreed that we could stretch this phase out a bit. Let's say from 1986-1992, round about the time we went off on a Somerset/Devon Tour. In the storming phase, 'team members vie for position as they attempt to establish themselves and their status' and 'cliques and factions form, and there may be power struggles'. So that would take us neatly to the first time we asked The Farmer, The Accountant, The Breeder and The Land Agent to captain occasional weekday matches to keep them quiet, say in 1999. All this excellence was getting quite exhausting.

'Agreement and consensus largely forms around the team' in the norming phase. 'There is general respect for the leaders, and some tasks get shared around the team.' Again, we were delighted to hear about the 'respect' bit, and even more so at the idea of tasks being shared around the team. As if. OK, so we're not quite there yet after 25 years, but, when we are, we will be ready for the reforming phase ('focus on over-achieving goals' and 'the team knows clearly why it is doing what it is doing').

Ten years later, by the way, Tuckman came out with a fifth phase – adjourning, wherein the group gets broken up as the task is successfully completed. And that's the one we're all hanging in there for.

Captaincy is not for the faint-hearted, which was a shame as Mount Faint-Hearted was always the number one holiday spot for Tree-Hugger and me. The whole experience of captaining the very people who seemed to want to play cricket with us, brought out a strong sense of cultural fatalism in the pair of us, and we consequently drifted off into some quiet parallel universe of utterly pointless knowledge gathering. We continued by acquiring a discounted copy of Mike Brearley's The Art of Captaincy, where he breaks the whole thing down into a series of manageable chunks, and we tried to make it our bible. After all, the man that tamed Botham, and simultaneously brought back the Ashes to England in 1981, surely had a thing or two to offer us. Not, necessarily, as it turned out.

As with the real Bible, we only read the exciting bits, of which there were none, and turned instead to the pictures. Clearly much of what he writes is not applicable to a club like ours (eg working with a coach, developing players as individuals, playing competent games of cricket or winning matches), so we developed our own take on some of his headings.

1. *Selecting a team and dealing with selection issues*: Traditionally, we have never needed to select a team, as we never have had enough volunteers to select from. More normally, The Hunter guide to captaincy would include techniques for persuading players that they wanted to play at the last minute rather than clear their garages, and a long list of people who we've met at social functions who said they might fancy a game one day, and why don't we give them a call if we really need someone at short notice. We often call, and they never

come. We would be much better off paying for all of our regulars to go on assertiveness courses, in order that they can more effectively pave the way with their other halves for permission to have the afternoon off.

The nearest we tend to get to a selection issue is when the match organiser has miscounted, and twelve players turn up. An embarrassing silence normally ensues, as the eleven who are not captaining wonder silently how the man who created the mess is going to sort it out. Normally, we ask the opposing skipper if we can play twelve, or we hope that he has only got ten and we can give him one of ours.

On one occasion, we played twelve without ever noticing it ourselves, until the moment when ten wickets had gone down in the second innings, and there was still someone to come in.

2. *Gaining respect as a captain*: Unlike Brearley, I have found that the surest way to gain my players' respect is to stay at home on match days. If I can't do this, then avoiding batting, bowling or fielding close to the wicket normally helps. Failing that, doing and saying as little as possible ticks most boxes. Then my contributions can be limited to appearing to have a grand plan, and seeming confident enough to execute it. Much can be achieved by looking the part, too, which is a shame as I don't.

The manner in which a captain handles tricky situations can add to, or subtract from, the respect he is held in. He must know how to handle difficult characters, how to calm down a developing row and how to nominate who is going to nip in from the outfield to put the urn on for tea. Every now and again, he might even go so far as to call back an opposing batsman who has been the victim of an appalling miscarriage of justice by his own umpiring colleague.

3. *Communication*: We communicate most pre-match stuff now by e-mail which works well apart from with The Poet who never checks his e-mails, and no longer seems even to have an account. Here, the captain must be at the same time authoritative enough to make something happen, and persuasive enough to allow people to think they will enjoy the match. He needs to get the venue right, the start time, the team list and the pub to meet at beforehand. He also needs to remember where the kit-bag was last seen, and ensure that someone brings it along. I am not aware that Mike Brearley ever had to frantically call around his Middlesex colleagues to see who had got the kit, or whether anyone had purchased a match ball.

On the field of play, he must communicate firmly but positively, only throwing his toys out of the pram afterwards in the privacy of his own car. Sometimes, he must accept that men of a certain age need everything to be told to them twice, and that in consequence of this, he will begin to sound like some faded Gilbert and Sullivan chorus. Finally, he must recognise that point in the match where the team's collective server has gone down, and all messages are being returned unopened. At that point, he needs to just go with the flow, and take up prescription narcotics instead.

Occasionally, all that holds us together is local geography, with a collective loathing of Bono thrown in for good measure.

4. ***Reading conditions***: Actually, all club pitches play roughly the same, but it looks good for captains to talk knowledgeably about conditions. In reality, all pitches tend to be more or less identical. They are 22 yards long, (other than the one match when The Tree Hugger managed to put the stumps in the wrong place,) 4 yards wide, greeny-brown and quite pretty. They have stumps at both ends and white lines in certain places. When they are wet, they are soggy, and when they are dry, they are bouncy. When it is sunny, they're warm, and when it's windy, they're cold. When it snows you can't see them. It's really not complicated. Early in a match, pitches are quite tidy, whereas later on they get a bit messy. Finally, when Tony Greig is commentating, they are full of little key-holes. Conditions are therefore always the same. Really, the way people complicate these things.

5. ***Applying appropriate tactics***: Again, this tends to be an over-worked concept, so slight is our technical ability to influence outcomes. After all, if the opposition is on the rack at 285-1, there's not a whole heap you can actually do about it. Therefore the tactics we play are the ones of mind games. When a batsman is well set, for example, The Human Sieve will often go into a long monologue on the state of the country to no one in particular, starting after each ball has been bowled and stopping just when the bowler is on his next run-up. Occasionally, but often enough for it to be worth it, the batsman will simultaneously lose his concentration, temper and wicket. When a fast bowler is tearing through your side, he needs frequently to be stopped in his own run-up for your batsman to walk up the pitch and collect an imaginary divot. Again, he may well start to spray it around in his irritation. If an opposition umpire gives a controversial decision against one of his own side, praise him publicly, and tell him loudly that you admire his sportsmanship. The possibilities are endless.

6. ***Knowing when to declare***: We have only declared once in 278 matches stretching over 25 years, so I'm not certain this is one of our major issues. I'll be sure and call Mike Brearley for advice if we ever get there again.

7. ***Knowing when to say 'no'***: As Lenin eventually found out, you can easily damage your outcomes by taking equality to extremes, and a captain needs to know when

and where to draw the line. Some players, for example, should never bowl. Ever. I almost keep putting myself in this category but two things stop me – my innate optimism, and the true awfulness of The Grenadier in this department. From his occupation, you would think that The Grenadier knew how to throw things accurately, added to which he learned his cricket properly, and is an elegant and calm batsman. But put a ball in his hands, and something snaps. You can see him running North to bowl just at the point that his co-ordination is sprinting South to the pavilion for an extended tea-break. At the moment of release, the ball rises slowly and vertically like a hot air balloon on a still summer's day, before coming to rest apologetically three feet to the left of the non-striking batsman. And it doesn't just do this exceptionally; it does this every time he bowls. The first man to touch it is normally fielding at mid-off. The Charity Worker does much the same. By the same token, The IT Man should never be allowed to take part in a chase for quick runs, and The Financial Adviser should never be asked to 'hold an end up'.

Like the old drug awareness advertisement says: 'Just say no'.

8. ***Setting the field***: This is the most public issue, and the one with the biggest potential for getting the opprobrium of your team-mates if you cock it up. Knowing that the ball will always go where the fielder isn't, the

real key is for the field to look right, rather than be right. Keith Miller, the one-time Australian skipper just told his players to 'scatter' as they came out of the pavilion, something I would cheerfully do if I didn't already know that they would all end up at first slip. Apart from anything, this approach allows the captain not to get caught out by his ignorance of where certain fielding positions actually are. I get around momentary lapses of memory by just pointing at blank pieces of grass and politely asking someone to 'just go there'.

So I tend to populate the outfield first (with anyone who can actually throw the ball), and then put anyone who is left in a circle close enough to prevent a single if the ball actually hits them on its way out. Placing three slips is a good way of nerving up a new batsman, but it only works before the ball is bowled. We hide our worst fielders at third man or fine leg, which creates much ongoing demand for those two positions. Finally, when I captain, I like to field at mid-on. This is not for any notion that I can actually control the game from there, but because it is quite a sociable place where human traffic seems to be happy to pass the time of day between overs. Also, the ball seems to arrive there rather slower than it does at mid-off.

As a team, we tend to change field placings in moody reaction to things that are happening to us, rather than in anticipation of them.

The Farmer invented a noise of ambulance sirens to be used when a captain had reacted to something too late, and this gets used by all-comers now, at times when the air is alive with the sounds of stable doors being slammed shut whilst horses hooves clatter off into the night.

9. *Controlling the order of things*: Later on, we'll go through how to devise a batting order. But there are other sequences, too. Who bowls when, for example, and who takes over from The Human Sieve when he goes off for a protracted comfort break. When someone puts the urn on for tea, when the sandwiches are put out, and when play starts again after the interval. Just as the natural state of an aircraft is to plough into the ground in default of firm human control, the natural state of a cricket match is to become a random sequence of cosmic events. Someone needs to keep it all going. Like it or not, that someone is the captain.

10. *Keeping everyone happy*: The great leadership guru never wrote about this, did he? The foremost role of a White Hunter skipper is to send everyone home happy, or as happy as a man can be after making a duck, not being asked to bowl and dropping three catches in a 9 wicket defeat. Each player must be treated as an individual. For example, The Farmer needs to be consulted ball after ball, and his jokes must be seen to be appreciated. Everyone knows that The Breeder's first over will

go for 16, but that he will settle down if he gets a few more, and if everyone is nice to him. Equally, The Investor needs to be given all four of his overs in one go, or his back seizes up and he is able to take no further part in the match. The Charity Worker is inscrutable, and must never be rushed. The Poet needs to be kept close to the action, as he goes into a creative vacuum if he is left on his own on the boundary. The Major is happy to be the comic centre of things, but his Tourettes Syndrome means that it is advisable to make him field in the deep, on the opposite side from the pavilion, miles away from the watching families. The Private Client, who regards a cricket match as no more than a semi-colon between the more substantial parts of his social life, simply requires to be kept in a good enough condition to bat somewhere at the top of the order. Something for everyone, and everyone treated as a something.

11. ***Running the Club bank account***: Another one that Messrs Brearley, Vaughan, Ponting and Strauss don't seem to have been troubled with, and a responsibility that doesn't even get a mention in Mr Brearley's little book. Every now and then, we try to appoint an Hon Treasurer from the ranks of our members with a financial background, but it doesn't work out. Suddenly, they're all too busy taking the banking system to the brink of collapse and back, and wouldn't want to risk the national finances by doing that tiny extra bit of work. They can grasp hedge funds, put options and

commodity tracking all right, but they take fright at the thought of being responsible for the cheques, a small bank account and a Rymans paperback double-entry account book. Besides, they always add, you two have made such a good job of it yourselves over the years. So the grubby cheque book goes from match to match, cohabiting in the kit-bag with Mr Masons's left-handed solo glove, and producing £0.02p of interest each year.

Only once did it all go wrong, when Tree-Hugger and I both thought that the other one had banked the cheques for the Oxfordshire Tour, when neither had. That week-end, we spent merrily on the Club's behalf, congratulating ourselves on the unprecedented levels of organisation that had got us here. It was not until the Monday morning when we got an agonised call from the manager of the Windsor Branch of Nat West, telling us that we were £300 overdrawn, and that, as signatories, we were personally responsible. Worse still, we had bounced a cheque in the sports shop in Winchester, which happened to be owned and run by the captain of one of our key opponents. The incident still gets mentioned every time we go in to buy a new box, even though decades have passed since it happened. The bundle of cheques was finally found under a pile of old cricket balls on a shelf in our pavilion.

The defining captaincy challenge for us both, of course, is that we are each routinely leading ten people who are better at cricket than the men leading them. Better at batting, at bowling, at fielding and probably at tactics. Some captains could be pulled down by all this, and accept that it will be fate and not they who will influence the outcome. Then they just wander off to hunker down in a miserable heap a mile or so beyond deep long on. Not I. For although I sometimes have the sensation of being a round peg in a square hole that isn't even there, I also begin to understand that there is a mystic element to my role in the team. It turns out that I am not expected to bat well, bowl well, field well or be brilliant at tactics. It is quite sufficient that I have organised the match and produced a batting order of sorts. Beyond that, I am simply a lightning conductor that people can look to and blame when it all goes tits-up. All that is required of me, in football-speak parlance, is that I stick my hand up when the chips are down. Quite where I stick it is a matter for conjecture, but so long as it is up rather than down, all is well.

For the other ten members of the team, it's rather like waking up one morning in 1942 somewhere in an Eighth Army encampment in Libya, and discovering that Winston Churchill has sent the Two Fat Ladies to take over from Montgomery. They just have to hope that there is enough momentum, and enough tanks, planes and competent soldiers to make the new Field Marshals irrelevant.

The source of endless fascination, though, is how Tree-Hugger and I appear to have occasionally evolved as more than the sum of our incompetence in the captaincy game.

Much of this comes down to knowing who to consult, when to consult them, and what to do with the advice. Some Hunters love to be consulted, like The Land Agent, The Investor and The Farmer. Others, like The Sieve, want no part of it. Some offer advice, called-for or not, either by shouting it unhelpfully from the deep, or by wandering up conspiratorially in between overs. Good captains always know what to do with the advice, even on the occasions when following it up would require an extremely technical visit to Accident and Emergency.

In our early days, we had more than our fair share of spare leaders. For all I know, Sandhurst runs courses in spare leadership, for those who want all the fun of telling people what to do without the inconvenience of taking the blame when it goes wrong. The spare leader is always close to the action. He has a shadowy opinion on every matter connected with the game. He has strong views on the batting order, but melts away when these are actively sought. He knows which bowler should come out at each stage of the match, but is always Macavity-like in his absence when you want his advice directly. He would almost certainly have taken that catch you just spilled, as well. His body language screams out over the outfield that each decision you make is wrong and inexplicable. Then one day, in frustration at the unspoken running commentary on your leadership, you ask him directly: 'what would you do?' 'Me?', he asks incredibly, 'Good Lord. I wouldn't know'. A particular joy of the last decade has been the gradual extinction of the spare leader from the club.

I also derive some satisfaction from walking back to a good young bowler's mark with him looking to all the world as if I am giving him advice. I'm not, of course, as I have no advice that I could possibly give. Also, if I tried, I would quite rightly be told where to stick it, on the basis of my profound ignorance, and the fact that I am one of the worst bowlers in the Northern Hemisphere. So I am actually saying something that has got nothing to do with cricket, but is designed to look like an embryonic plan. The idea is that the batsman then worries himself into doing something stupid, and thus surrenders his wicket. So long as I never bowl a ball myself, it is fine, and the unwary batsman at the striker's end might, just possibly might, think that he is the unwilling target of a web of subtle intrigue.

The same technique applies to batting. Because they do it on the telly, I have spent 25 years wandering down the wicket in between overs to say some platitude to the batsman out there with me. Every now and again, normally when there is a teenager resident at the other end, we will touch gloves in celebration of the fact that we have just seen off another three balls. With most, the conversation will be a choice of two or three things: 'we can get there in singles'; 'just play your natural game'; or 'you stay here, and I'll hit up'. With The Sieve or The Farmer, it tends to be a piece of social realism, although The Sieve is rarely around long enough for a meaningful conversation to develop. With The Investor, it might actually be on the subject of the cricket game in progress, unlikely though that may seem. With The Charity Worker and The Financial Adviser it tends to be more along the lines of how far up their colon my bat will end if they run me out again.

There are also all those burdensome responsibilities of health and safety/discrimination legislation that a captain must consider these days, and we have had hours of fun in this respect. From the outset, we wanted to ensure that the White Hunters was a cricket club that offered equal opportunities to all, regardless of race, religion, colour, sexual orientation or ability. Above all, ability. The fact that the majority of the team appeared to the untrained eye to be drawn from able-bodied, straight, white, Anglo-Saxon Protestants masked the fact that we went to the ends of the earth to bring in players with no ability, and all the co-ordination of a dead muskrat. From time to time we attempted to recruit West Indians and Sri Lankans to the cause, but they were having none of it. A West Indian of average ability has much better things to do with his time of a Saturday afternoon, than participating in what we like to call competitive cricket.

The antithesis of this captaincy lark lies also, of course, in just how indecisive some of our best cricketers can be once they are handed over the reins themselves. Tree-Hugger and I began to share out the captaincy duties with others after about fifteen or so years, spurred on by the fact that

a) we weren't very good at it ourselves and b) the captain has the sometimes onerous duties of getting a team together and organising things with the opposition. Thus, it often turns out that the man who only last weekend was putting The Hammer Bottom Butser's attack to the sword, can easily be reduced to a gibbering wreck by the responsibilities of office. He can work himself into a clinical depression by something as simple as thinking through the fielding positions, let alone who bats and bowls when. He will either worry too much that he has offended someone, or genuinely offend someone by not worrying enough about them. Invariably, he will try to be too polite with his team, and equally invariably, this engaging attribute will get him precisely nowhere. He will tend to leave bowlers on too long when they are being hit around, whilst simultaneously positioning himself deeper and deeper in the outfield until the point when his presence is a mere atomic signature, a subliminal memory somewhere in the outer reaches of our universe. Above all, his own performance with bat and ball will crumble. As Gerry Adams probably knows by now, true satisfaction arises from sticking to what you are good at.

When all the peripheral stuff is de-constructed, the captain is simply the conductor of the orchestra, dependent on the First Violin, the Double Bass and their assorted colleagues. If the captain is a bastard, everyone will eventually leave. If he tries to please everyone, on the other hand, he will end up pleasing no one at all. If, however, he is quirky, enthusiastic and resolute, there is just a small chance that people will follow him, probably only out of curiosity, in default of anything better to do with themselves. Many years later, Mike Brearley's book is propping up a work-bench in my potting shed and Leadership in Organisations got given to the Petworth Womens' Institute book sale, where it remained unsold.

To an extent, though, the old saying is right. The higher a monkey goes up the tree, the more he reveals of himself. The really sensible White Hunters are quite content to let others climb, and just remain at the base feeding on the falling nuts.

Chapter 9

UNBEATEN SOUTH OF THE LOIRE: THE 2000 FRENCH TOUR

'If the French noblesse had been capable of playing cricket with their peasants, their chateaux would never have been burned.' GM Trevelyan

It was the wild boar that started it, and not us. However, no one could argue that it wasn't us that finished it off.

The boar's creator had given him free will to decide whether or not it was a good move to run across the dark Normandy road on that early September morning in front of the speeding team minibus. He simply chose wrong. There was a loud thud, a momentary possibility that the bus would roll over, and then silence.

The Land Agent and I marched back fifty metres or so through the mist to the point where the life blood was oozing out of the boar, and concluded inevitably that the creature had to be humanely dispatched. With a pheasant or rabbit, this is of course the work of a quick sleight of hand, but a wild boar presented a trickier challenge altogether. Searching round for a weapon with which to deliver the coup de grace, it suddenly became blindingly obvious what was required.

'Get a cricket bat,' someone said. And we did. And so it was that a farmer from the locality, breasted the hill in his dark Citroen 2CV and saw two strange adult men repeatedly hitting a prostrate wild boar with their cricket bats in the roadside verge of a route national. It was possibly not the Club's finest hour and certainly not the wild boar's. Once the thing had been pronounced dead by our own two experts, The Farmer and The Breeder, we debated for a few minutes as to whether we should sit it on the front seat of the minibus with a safety belt, club sweater and cap on, just to see if the douaniers at Cherbourg were as switched on as they should be. After all, we had failed to take out a collision damage waiver on the rental, and, in compensation, we felt that we could get a sod of a lot of sausages out of a wild boar. Selling the sausages might go some way towards paying off the rather steep excess we were likely to incur. The French farmer settled matters by opening the tiny boot of his 2CV and folding the boar inelegantly in. He had a face that only a mother could love, and smelled faintly of stereotypes.

'Allez, et bon retour!', he said, indicating that it was the least he could do for us, and that the conversation was now at an end. He waved a Gallic hand back at us before spluttering off into the dawn. For our part, we spent much of the wait for the ferry re-fashioning the front bumper to make it seem, at a cursory glance from the Hire Company staff at any rate, that nothing was amiss.

In hindsight, The Tree-Hugger might have had more energy to concentrate on his driving, had he not spent the last 72 hours trying to evade the homo-erotic fancies of one of the locals. Unlikely as it may seem, and this is up there with the chances of finding intelligent life at Lords, Tree-Hugger had become the target of the repeated advances of a bizarre local landowner. And possibly the whole team might have been less nervous had dinner on the first night not ended with the host throwing kitchen knives into the panelled walls of the dining room. He had walked in to find a couple of us guiltily hiding the fact that we had been trying to throw clementines through some of the missing panels of leaded lights, and had insisted that real boys games should be much tougher than that. We had no idea just how much tougher he meant. There was a strange imperative we all suddenly felt to be somewhere else, with someone else, and in the next five minutes.

What it all boils down to is that most teams don't tour for personal enjoyment, but rather to fill up the anecdote reservoir for the next few seasons. Stories arise that can be offered time and again, honed, altered, exaggerated, re-fashioned and burnished up until they gleam like a lantern on the moors. For some mildly depressing reason, tours require later members of the club to have to go through an apprenticeship of wildly exaggerated in-jokes and tall stories, before they can feel themselves to be a real part of things. This can be quite wearing. The White Hunters, on the other hand, tour for all the best and most selfless reasons, such as giving our families a break from us, and bringing a great sport to a hitherto benighted and savage people who would not otherwise ever see it.

Hence France.

We had arranged to go there for the Millennium Tour because we were frankly fed up with losing. The land of de Gaulle could boast 460 different cheeses, a 35 hour week and more strikes than you would get in a beginner's base-ball game, but it couldn't even run to publishing Wisden in its own language. These people needed help. Our help. Besides, it stood to reason that, if you went to a country that didn't play cricket, (and even better, served agreeable food and wine) you would not be beaten. Er, well not quite.

The usual suspects lined up to join the tour, and the possible inclusion of wives and girlfriends was vigorously debated, as it has been before every tour we have ever done. It is a debate with the same predictable outcome each time it is held. Whether they were invited along or not, it turned out, their men would be required to lay on rather more in the way of sunshine, ancient monuments and nice shops, and rather less in the way of matting wickets, cheap accommodation and rubbish anecdotes. Incidents like the wild boar and the knife throwing wouldn't help future recruitment, either. We have been given a standing order of 'no, thank you', therefore, until we put together a long weekend of cricket in Venice, Florence or Barcelona.

We had trained to a hair, even to the extent of producing a user-friendly sheet of translations for the technical terms we might need to explain to our hosts:

English	French
White Hunter	*Chasseur blanc*
Win the toss	*Gagne le ballotment*
We are fielding	*Nous champons*
Sledge	*Luge*
Wide	*Vaste*
Wrong 'un	*Faux un*
Wicket-keeper	*Gardien de guichet*
Howzat	*Ca va?*
Slip	*Négligé*
New ball	*Testicule nouveau*

Gully	*Ravine*
Pads	*Tampons*
Third man	*Troisiéme homme*
Golden Duck	*Canard d'or*
Cover	*Couverture*
Deep cover	*Couverture profonde*
Bye	*Au revoir*
Leg Bye	*Jambe au revoir*
Fine Leg	*Jambe splendide*
Looks plum from here	*Il regarde un prune d'ici*
Long stop	*Ârret longue*
Oh, for Goodness sake	*Pour l'amour de Dieu*
Silly mid-off	*Milieu dessus stupide*
Sticky dog	*Chien adhesive*
Cow corner	*Coin de la vache*
Bowler	*Chapeau formel*
Maiden over	*Jeune fille finis*
Sorry, Mark	*Pardon, Mark*
Long hop	*Cloche-pied longue*
Square leg	*Jambe traditionelle*
I think it's my hamstring	*Je pense que c'est ma ficelle de jambon*
He turned that a mile	*Il l'a tourné 1.609 kilometres*
I was trying the reverse sweep	*J'essayait le draggage de retour*
Bang goes my average	*La détonation de mon moyen*

I haven't come all this way to be given out LBW

Merde

We were promised a feast of weekend cricket in the Loire

Valley, starting in the old Military Cavalry town of Saumur, which happens to boast one of the few grass strips in all of France. In the event, it turned out that the gentleman who had promised us a feast was clearly satisfied with extremely small meals. Not for the last time in our existence, the research phase of an operation had let us down.

We arrived at the first pitch fresh from the Saturday prix fixe lunch menu at some sunlit riverside bistro. For some reason, we had got it into our heads that the opposition would consist largely of men called Jean-Philippe or Didier, and that they would probably turn up in stripey shirts on old black bicycles festooned with strings of onions. Furthermore, we rather fancied that they would be no match for us, and that for the first time in fourteen years of trying, we could dominate and bully a team the way the Australians did. We quite fancied doing a bit of bullying, as it happened, and The Major spent a good deal of the journey telling us how it was going to be when we got there. It didn't quite work out that way. I got an inkling that it might not, when the first person who shook my hand introduced himself as Tendulkar.

'No relation, I hope!' I laughed. He indicated that he was, but only distantly through the Chennai Tendulkars. He also started to introduce me to what turned out to be a large selection of Mick Jagger's house staff from the area: two Australians, a New Zealander, a West Indian, a Sri Lankan, four Brits, an Italian and – eventually – a solo Frenchman.

'We thought that this would be a French team,' Tree-Hugger offered rather lamely at the toss.

'God no,' said the skipper. 'We'd be buggered in the league if we had Frenchmen.'

The notion of a whole heap of colonial gladiators and a league simply hadn't entered into our calculations, probably in the same way as the notion of a bunch of disorientated losers hadn't entered theirs. We underwent that familiar sinking feeling we tend to get when we are watching athletic twenty somethings climb out of vans with coffins full of well-used kit, and determined glints in their eyes. Many years later the same sort of thing happened to us at Toulouse. Far from being proud Gascons to a man, the team that decanted from the minibus to play us all appeared to be on the payroll of Airbus, whose Headquarters were just down the road, and most of them had learned their cricket in Bombay or Columbo, rather than Bordeaux or Carcasonne.

A long tradition of sporting cliché obliges me to say that, for a time, we punched above our weight in the match. We batted first, and Tree Hugger and The Recruitment Consultant harvested a careful 19 runs for the first wicket, to which were added a much more robust 14 from The Major. The Farmer and I contributed to a partnership of 35 in our varying styles, and so we went on down the order.

It was rather touching to see the complete disinterest with which the local dog walkers and joggers appeared to view proceedings. After all, if you found a group of people on Hampstead Heath in berets playing petanque, you might well stop and stare for a moment or two. Or, come to think of it, on Hampstead Heath you might not. But the people walking round the ground were staring ahead with glassy-eyed determination, rather like someone might do if a large and ugly person was removing all their clothes on the platform at Euston Station. Best to ignore it, dear, don't stare, but move quickly on.

A decade later, only two things remain instantly memorable from our efforts in Saumur. First, the Poet's bowling analysis of 2 overs, 1 maiden, 23 runs, 1 wicket. Secondly, it was at Saumur that The Journalist started nurdling in earnest. No Hunter had ever nurdled anything before, and here was someone building an entire innings on the concept. He nurdled to the extent that one of the Australian bowlers started questioning first his skill, and then his parentage. The score-book records only that he nurdled his way to 12 in the end, but what a 12! Each run was crafted with infinite patience from soft hands and a loosely angled bat somewhere between first and second slip. If he faced six balls in an over, he was quite content to let five of them go straight to slip, so long as the sixth squeezed through the gap and gained him a run. This was rare excellence, and we were all rather proud of it. It was one of the very few times that a White Hunter had pre-mediated something deliberately, let alone executed it. (In his day job, he was covering the final rowing events from the Sydney Olympics on behalf of a major national newspaper, which happened to be taking place that very weekend. Quite whether the bedroom of a chateau in the Loire Valley was the perfect place to give informed views of the competition, I wouldn't know and couldn't say).

Saumur, having been set 157 to win, sent in a tall white Australian and a short black Englishman. Looking back at it now, I'm not sure what put it into our minds that they had reversed the batting order, but, whatever they had done, there was something rather awesome about what happened next.

There was one tidy over from The Breeder, which acted as a calm before the storm, after which the short black Englishman simply tore into us, scoring 100 not out off the 56 balls he faced. In the context of a target of 156, this was a disappointing outcome for the fielding side. No one else from Saumur really got amongst us, but then they didn't need to. Mr Johnson was doing it for them. It didn't matter what we bowled at him, he just hit it back harder. It didn't matter who shared the pain of bowling at him, he simply took to it even quicker than he had to the previous one. To be fair to him, he had an apologetic, almost sad air about him throughout the innings, like a philosopher who after a lifetime of effort has discovered, and then suddenly mislaid, the true meaning of life. We came to the conclusion that he was probably running late for an important wine tasting event, but didn't want to let his team mates down by leaving the ground early. Wickets were falling at the other end for not many individual runs, but Johnson seemed oblivious to it all.

In all, by the time they reached their victory target, it had taken Saumur 18 overs to knock off what we had taken 40 to build, and we hadn't even played that badly.

As we trooped off the field, a moth-eaten local dog limped on to the square and proceeded to extrude a large turd where The Farmer had been keeping wicket only seconds before. It seemed to sum up what had just happened to us.

'No matter', said The Tree-Hugger to no one in particular, as we bundled the kit into the minibus. 'We're still unbeaten south of the Loire'. (A decade later we contrived to lose two consecutive games in Gascony, meaning that, whilst we have still never won a cricket match in France, we remain unbeaten south of Toulouse.)

Sunday's match didn't even make it into our score-book, mainly because our host had omitted a) to organise it b) to tell us he hadn't really got a pitch at all and c) to let us know that he didn't have an opposition either. What he did have was a field somewhere near the Chateau, that made Apple-treewick look like a bowling green, and a few big hearted neighbours who came along to see what all the fuss was about. With the Autumn sun warming our backs, a tributary of the Loire lapping around the edge of the field, and a heady mix of Muscadet and Anjou wines swilling around in our bodies, we felt it would have been churlish to grouse about it, and worse still to have refused to play. If this was what a cricket tour to France amounted to, then who were we to complain?

We split our own team 6-5, and then added the interested locals in inverse proportion so as to make two teams, where at least half the players had some technical knowledge of the game. Whilst this was not quite what we had envisaged when we had set out for France, it seemed strangely in keeping with the way we did things. Besides, it had the added advantage that, technically at least, we could avoid two defeats on our first ever French tour, never an unimportant consideration for the team.

The Land Agent and The Journalist set themselves up as the de facto coaches, and a succession of bewildered but cheerful Frenchmen came through to learn what this was all about. It probably would have been a lot easier if we had told them just to hit the red ball with the brown stick, rather than what we actually did, which was to try to translate all the intricate terms and fielding positions into their language.

The huge danger of this kind of beer match is that shame devolves onto specific individuals rather than the team.

Being someone who likes to shelter under the umbrella of a rubbish team performance, I find it is much safer on these occasions to volunteer to bat at 11, not to bowl at all, and to field somewhere in the deep. That way, nothing untoward can happen to make you appear even more incompetent than you really are. Although the over-riding temptation is to think how good it would be for your average to score a quick 50 not out, and take three quick wickets, life does not work like that. When you come in, after years of playing the game, to face a farm-worker called Yves who hadn't even heard of it until eleven o'clock that morning, you have little to gain and much to lose.

Personally, I was stumped early in my innings by The Farmer, bowled (off a wide) by someone called Ricard. I had got it into my head that something three feet outside my off stump represented a scoring opportunity, rather than the self-inflicted time bomb it really was, with all the potential venom of a Green Mamba. I stepped across to connect with it, and thus altered my centre of gravity just enough to fall over about a foot and a half from where I was supposed to be, with the inevitable consequence of dismissal. And when Yves' father-in-law came out to face the searing pace of The Poet, and smacked him back over his head for a cross-batted six into the adjacent stubble, The Poet came as close as a mild-mannered man of art can come, to sledging him in his own language. Only he didn't know that 'Luge' was the French for sledge, and passed up the opportunity.

Things progressed in this sultry and Autumnal way until

The Host came in to bat. Whilst not going so far as to dislike the man, our feelings about him by this stage were slightly equivocal, on the basis that what he had actually provided bore only a very passing resemblance to what had been promised (and paid for) in the glossy brochure five months before. But he was a genial man who wanted us to have a good time.

In the event, he lasted two balls. He made a huge song and dance of taking guard where the crease might have been if anyone had bothered to mark it out, and an even greater one of clocking all the fielding positions. He greeted those around him as long-lost friends, chuckling away about the excellence of it all. The first ball he studiously patted back to the bowler. The second, bowled by the rampant Breeder, reared up off the dried out remnants of a cow pat, and struck The Host half way between his jaw and his open mouth. Two teeth came out on the pitch, and another two looked set to follow once the next baguette was introduced. The Host headed off to hospital, bloody, in some pain, but much consoled that it seemed to provide amusement for everyone else.

Which brings us back to the dead boar, to the insurance excess on our minibus and to the long journey home.

Chapter 10

HOME

'Home is not where you live,
but where they understand you'
Christian Morgenstern

All of this travel and dead wildlife could easily mask the fact that most of our cricket is played within a few miles of Winchester.

We are nothing if not sedentary, even parochial, creatures, whose every summer instinct is to drift quietly along the A272 towards our Saturday afternoon match, cursing the sound quality of the Long Wave Test Match Special broadcast. The Yacht Designer doesn't even drift along the A272, as he already lives over the shop. Others head off to weekend retreats in the Gorges de Tarn, or buy a family queue-buster ticket to some Experience or other, but the Hunters rarely stray far from the South Downs. This is because the South Downs are home, and having a physical home is probably one of the key reasons why the team still exists as something more concrete than a distant memory. Having a beautiful home has allowed us to be much less competent than we should have been, and yet still worth keeping on opposition fixture lists.

We were once homeless. In our early seasons, we wandered nomadically from venue to venue, like a caravan of disabled Biblical shepherds, always conscious that we were utterly reliant on the current opposition finding something sufficiently quirky or attractive in us, to justify asking us back again. And, whilst we did quirky pretty effectively, we were much less strong on doing attractive. The Farmer did a nice forward defensive push, to be sure, and The Poet had an alluring way of brushing his locks away from his face in between deliveries, but there was nothing concrete there that we could hang our hat on. In truth, we were in danger of becoming one of those teams that play one match a year and then die quietly after a violent post-match disagreement in a pub because the necessary glue isn't there to bind it all together.

Then something wonderful happened. In the lead up to a local match in 1989, some heavy rain leaked under the covers of the pitch we were due to play. Having been cancelled, we were doing those disconsolate things you do when you realise that a match isn't going to happen, which included telling all the players. One of these was The Groundsman, and his reply rather surprised us.

'Oh, you can always have mine, if you want.'

Now, if you lose a football, or a penknife or something, that would be quite a plausible answer. But if it's a cricket pitch you've mislaid, you can't really expect the second person you communicate with to have one of their own. And not only one of their own, but one of an extraordinary standard. And then to want you to use it. But the offer was there, large as life, and we weren't suddenly going to spoil it by having a Uriah Heep hand-wringing 'No, we couldn't possibly impose ourselves on you like that' moment afterwards. (Anyway, if we were looking for a Dickensian character to epitomise a White Hunter, it would be more of a Mr Micawber, always waiting for something to turn up).

'Yes, please,' one of us said, and it has remained said for the next twenty-three years.

The thing about 'home' is that you belong there. It is where you are surrounded by familiar people and things, and where you are, if not appreciated, then tolerated for what you are. It is where you can one moment be the wit and motivator of a team, and the next be just another failed batsman, miserable because the ball 'quite clearly hit the bat'. There, the sun traces a familiar arc across the sky each time you visit, and the local trees stand as the basic comforting architecture of the surrounding countryside. Shrubs grow discreetly from year to year in the background, in sympathy with waistlines, the scarlet of their flowers matching the occasional visiting nose. A man could get quite overcome with it all if he didn't know better.

The ground is a large square with the south-western corner chewed out of it by a barn and car park, a feature that brings the fine leg boundary unusually close to the action. It takes most visiting teams a year or two to understand that, whatever the state of the game, you need a fielder on the apex of this point. And I'm not talking about one of those larger than life static ones, like The Major, who beams genially at things going on around them, and moving past them, but never move and can't throw. I'm talking about a wafer thin racing snake who can cover 100 metres in about 9.6 seconds, and has an arm like a rapier. So not me, then, either. Possibly The Accountant, but definitely not me.

We are surrounded on two sides, if you can be surrounded on two sides, by a chunk of mature mixed woodland. It's the kind of place that harbours Japanese snipers for fifty years or so, and, certainly, someone called Harvey wandered off into it to relieve himself during a match in 1996 and never came back. Otherwise, it is rarely visited, except when The Yacht Designer is bowling, when it gets visited surprisingly often.

The Yacht Designer lives in a barn adjacent to the ground, and he has come increasingly to support The Groundsman in enabling us to stay there, and play there, by helping out with the donkey work needed to keep it all going. If skill and results reflected the amount of hours and effort put in to playing and practising the game, then The Yacht Designer would currently have a central contract with the ECB. He does nets all year round, and plays cricket indoors and outdoors all year round, too, presumably on the basis that January to December is normally quite a lean time in the yacht designing business. However, he does not have a central contract with the ECB because, however bare the cupboard, the ECB is not yet quite ready for his mysterious brand of ill-disguised slow non-turning long hops just outside off stump. Ball after ball, over after over, game after game, he weaves his magic spell; and game after game, opposition batsmen fill their boots, and make a mental note to come back to this run-fest until their ancient legs can no longer carry them. All that being said, lack of competition in the White Hunter spin department has meant that he is still some way from losing his place with us.

The other thing about home is that it happens to be the physical embodiment of how other sides view you. It is something of substance by which they can link the dry statistics in their scorebook with the warm feeling they have each year as they drive away. Matches fade in the memory as quick as the summer dew, as do individual innings, bowling spells and all but the best catches. Even the players who populate the ground are transitory, it turns out. Mythology might just sculpt some of them into marker posts by which you are able to measure the passing decades, but that's about it. In contrast, images of the ground never fade. Visitors seem to remember each detail, as the whole deal applies a magnetic attraction calling them back for more. They keep using the over-rated word 'special' when they talk about it, but, on this occasion, it is well-chosen.

Presiding over it all are The Groundsman and his wife, The Magistrate. For them, each match is more of a personal invitation into their family home than anything else. They do it, we sense, because they love what they have and, equally, love to share it with friends. For The Groundsman, the pitch has been more than a passion. I spent a year living in a house whose main bedroom overlooked the pitch, and only then realised quite what was involved in keeping it so apparently 'effortlessly' immaculate. It didn't seem to matter what time I got up and looked out, he was out there doing things to it. He might be mowing the square with a spotless Ransome, or preparing the outfield with an ancient gang mower. He could be painting the lines round the boundary or throwing seed out onto a bare patch. Whatever he was doing, the most animated thing about him would be his pipe moving gently up and down in his mouth, with its faint smoke signals rising up into the dawn of a hot summer's day.

In the early days, The Groundsman played in every match

himself. His two trademark shots are an eight iron chip over mid-wicket, or a lurch forward into delighted defence. His stock ball is a high lob out of the sun, and his standard fielding position is square leg. In fact, he will go nowhere else, and droit de seigneur allows him to be there for as long as he wants. Those of us who have played with The Groundsman for half a lifetime, can just about make out the physical hurt trace across his face when some oaf of a visiting batman takes divots out of the pitch. Otherwise he is a closed book.

Latterly, he has taken up serious motor sport, and he has a car to prove it. Actually, he has two cars. Whilst he doesn't play that much any more, we have been doubly lucky in that a) he has wanted us to stick around and b) The Yacht Designer has moved in next door and has helped to keep the whole thing going.

The Magistrate does the teas. She didn't always, but I think she noticed the complete bachelor mess that tended to get brought along, and decided that it would be a kindness to take the duty off our hands. Possibly it had something to do with standards, as well. She has many better things to do, but allows cricket to prevent her from doing them from time to time. She does much more than the teas, though, and we know it well. The unsaid deal is that we bring along agreeable teams who appreciate and respect the venue. The other part of the deal is that we don't bring along teams with dogs that terrorise the resident lop-eared rabbit, with children who throw gravel onto the pitch, or with captains who refuse to play a limited overs match, and subsequently instruct their batsmen to play for a tedious draw from the word go. Lining up to urinate against the barn wall after a trip to the pub doesn't go down that well, either.

By and large we manage to achieve satisfaction, and many of our regular oppositions have visited a dozen times or more. These tend to be like-minded people who we only see once or twice in a year, mostly getting older, larger and less mobile to exactly the same rhythm as us, and who are as amazed as we are that we are still allowed to be here. On the few occasions that we have misjudged an opposition, we have normally done the dirty deed and fired them long before we have had to be asked to. Indeed, oppositions tended to be judged in the early days on three criteria. Did they a) say nice things to The Groundsman, b) buy drinks in the pub afterwards and c) lose? If the answer to all three was 'yes, they were home and hosed for another invite.

At times, Home has been what has given the club the stimulus it needed to continue in existence. At the end of the 1998 season, the White Hunters had gone on the critical care list. Matches were increasingly difficult to fill, and those that were filled tended to be lost quickly. Many of the old guard had found other things to do with their time, and the players who replaced them hadn't really begun to make their presence felt. With a sense of hubris, Tree-Hugger and I wrote to anyone who had played over the course of the season, inviting them to an EGM (extremely genial meeting) to see if it was worth ploughing on. The section quoted below will strike a chord with anyone who has ever run a roving club side:

'One of the reasons for lacklustre performances (apart from lack of talent, overdrafts, hangovers and all the normal ones) is the difficulty we have found all summer in first raising, and then maintaining, a team of eleven players for any particular match. The hard core seems to have gone and, not to split hairs, so sometimes have the manners, enthusiasm and ability to stick to a plan. On one occasion, eighteen players were "recruited" (all said "yes" at some time) for the same match, to which ten actually bothered to turn up.

Once the foot-stamping and hair-tearing is over, we realise that this produces a genuine problem. If the club has run its course, (and if it should gently expire on a bed of nostalgia and dropped catches), it is most important that we know now so that alternate arrangements can be made for the ground. If the club still has mileage, and we still stubbornly believe it's fun, and that we might actually get better one day, we need to refresh a core commitment, and gauge how we can improve things for the membership'.

The meeting went ahead, initially with much uncertainty about the outcome. Then, as the evening wore on, and the pints disappeared into pits of echoing nostalgia, it became clear that the threat of losing the ground spoke louder than almost anything else we might be walking away from. It was something precious that we all suddenly came to realise was something we weren't prepared to lose. After all the months of messing around and letting ourselves down, it turned out that the glue that held us together as much as the affection we all felt for each other, was the place that we called Home.

Chapter 11

THE EVOLUTION OF WOMAN

On a fine summer day many people spend hours watching cricket matches. The women and girls wear pretty summer dresses, and the men and the boys take off their jackets. The spectators often eat ice cream and drink orangeade as they watch.
The Ladybird book of cricket (1964)

I once dreamed that I was in the basement of Cawdor Castle, trying to persuade Lady Macbeth to let her husband turn out for the White Hunters in our match against Goodwood the following day. Before giving her answer, she faded off into the shape of a haddock, and swum off to unload rifles from the dishwasher. My dreams are like that: they reflect some of my deepest anxieties. (Another one revolves around me being selected to play for England, forgetting my bat, borrowing someone else's, and then waiting in the rain for my turn to bat whilst the square gets smaller and smaller until it consists just of me and a bowler with a giant Dennis Lillee moustache.)

Macbeth would, I fancy, have been a gritty and grumpy middle order batsman along the lines of Jonathan Trott. The kind of man a team would collectively prefer not to take on tour because everything in the hotel would be wrong for him, and he would furtively order a decent bottle of wine at dinner, whilst everyone else was drinking house plonk. A man who would embark on a civil engineering project at his crease before each ball was bowled, and thus make the opposition want to do nothing more than injure him. And Lady Macbeth, more importantly, would have been one of those tricky wives, part of whose mission was to stop her husband enjoying himself, and part was simultaneously to try to get him into a more fashionable and high-achieving team. You can't really see her getting amongst the egg and cress sandwiches on the production line, either. She would probably limit herself to turning up once a year, and then spending the entire time monopolising the one good-looking member of the opposition.

What is it about women and cricket?

Personally, I think it all stems from the fundamental inability of most females to throw a cricket ball. Just as Nick

Clegg ultimately found out that a lifetime of preparing to harvest meaningless protest votes wasn't great preparation for a spell in government, so women stare bitterly from the long-on boundary, wishing that they could hurl the ball in like that 17 year old just did, but knowing deep down that it could never happen. I know, by the way, for I feel exactly the same. For most members of the female sex, it is this simple physical peculiarity that disenables them from getting stuck in to the sport. Local research indicates that it is also the hardness of the ball, coupled with the expectation that people are supposed to catch the thing that also puts them off.

This is because women trivialise sport, and too often try to boil it down to its lowest common denominator- whether you win or lose. They are not prepared to embrace the multi-layered dramas that men so welcome. They just don't understand, for example, that a painful injury taken in making a futile attempt to catch a fast moving hard round leather thing is sufficient glory of itself, and to be worried about whether or not it was actually caught is a matter for pedants, a simple question of semantics. Clearly, to boil cricket down to basics is counter-productive, as every man knows. You simply can't simplify things to this degree. You need to take into consideration hundreds of other factors, such as whether you looked good, whether what you did could later be cast in a plucky, heroic mould, even how many hours you spent afterwards discussing why you did what you did, and how much more spectacular history has made it than reality seemed to. Apparently it takes a male fully to understand these complexities.

This all seems strange, for women are actually demonstrably better than men at winning cricket matches. Fact. In 2009, England Women won the ICC's Women's World Cup at the North Sydney Oval by beating New Zealand by 4 wickets. This was the third time they had won this tournament, not to mention the three other times that they had been in the Finals, and they will probably go into the 2013 tournament as clear favourites. Compare and contrast this with the more celebrated, better-trained, better-paid men: often the bridesmaids (1979, 1987, 1992) but never, in ten times of asking, the bride. Women also fly high in the 20/20 form of the game, and aren't so bad at Test matches either.

In other words, English women are as good at, or better than, English men at cricket by almost every available yardstick and yet, outside the elite form of the game, it is still a sport whose gates are largely slammed in their faces at the age of 10. Count the number of times you have sat down to watch girls, or even a girl, playing the sport on a village green on a sunny summer's evening, and then ask yourself if they don't have the right to be fractionally pissed off. Possibly this is why they don't jump at the chance of dropping everything and coming to watch the boys strutting their stuff.

The White Hunters deal with this patent unfairness by, er, well, largely pretending it doesn't exist. From time to time in our history we have invited one of the spectators to replace an injured colleague, and have placed her in the safety of the slip cordon or down at fine leg. In nearly 300 matches, we have only started one of them with a girl on board, and that was, I seem to remember, that we were too scared to tell her that she couldn't do it. It has occasionally occurred to us that, as a team that has lost every match it has ever played in France (a country, in case you hadn't noticed, that does not play cricket), we should join a female league. After all, there would be less travel involved for similar achievement.

Anyone who knows anything about the British climate knows that conditions tend to be dryer and sunnier in the morning than they do in the afternoon. It's all to do with clouds building up in the heat of the day and then raining on people just after they have started doing something that requires them to be dry. Faced with this, you would think that all cricket games would start at about 8.30 a.m, and would be coming towards a conclusion by lunch time. The problem for men in this respect is that weekend mornings are for jobs, and the unspoken deal is that cricket can only start when the jobs have finished. Traditionally, this happens at about lunchtime, by which time the clouds have rolled in and the first duck of the day is eyeing up the wicket speculatively, and wondering to itself if there will be enough water there in a few hours' time for it to be considered a suitable nesting site. (It is also wondering if the Human Sieve will be along soon to keep it company, but that's another story.) If our maritime climate were more reliable, more consistently warm and sunny in the summer months, I rather fancy that our empty cricket grounds might have more in the way of female spectators. Therein lies problem number one.

This leads more or less directly to the second problem that girls have with cricket, namely their sense of disappointed idealism. Mythology has convinced them that cricket is a game to be played exclusively on dreamy country house grounds, where windless sunshine puts dappled shadows through the ancestral cedar trees. Their Corinthian husband shares an opening stand of 80 or so runs with David Gower, both drilling half volleys along the ground to the point boundary; tea, when it arrives, has been prepared by someone else, and comes in translucent bone china Spode cups, accompanied by the most delicate of sandwiches and cakes. The match ends when their triumphant other half celebrates his performance and her support by whisking her off to the Manoir au Quatre Saisons for a surprise dinner and an £800 suite thereafter.

Reality says different. Reality places them on a windswept hill-top ground hard by a high rise housing estate, where dark clouds scud across the sky, blowing the damp review section of their Sunday newspaper inside out, and making four layers, plus a cagoule for the regular showers, a necessity. Their man is out second ball, drops a sitter right in front of the pavilion and pulls up with a bad back half way through his first over. He remains too angry to speak for the rest of the day. Tea, which she has had to help purchase and produce because the skipper forgot that tiny detail altogether, consists of a plate of thick jam sandwiches, some squashed fly biscuits and a catering size bag of Doritos, and they then travel home in silence to a bubble and squeak from last night's mashed potato. Late in the evening, all she can hear is the clunking sound of a box going round and round in the tumble dryer, and all she can smell is the faint rot of a damp old club sweater. You can begin to see her point, and her point is that she has many better and more important things to do, and she has only come to the game to fulfil the 'worse', 'poorer' and 'sickness' parts of her marriage vows in one go.

This leads inexorably towards the third grievance that girls have with cricket, the fact that they always seem to get painted as the villains. Most excuses offered by men dropping out of a match imply that a degree of responsibility rests with their other half. This strikes me as quintessentially unfair for many reasons, starting with the fact that they probably forgot to tell her about the match in the first place. One of the reasons for the survival of the White Hunters, is that many, indeed most, of us had the good fortune to marry girls who at least tried to understand what this game was all about, and who accepted that it was important to us, and was therefore important to them by extension. Once the brush fires of machismo are beaten down into their smoky remnants, it is clear to anyone with eyes to see that we play cricket because of them, not in spite of them.

In turn, our part of the deal was threefold. We were not to expect them to come to any particular match, let alone all of them; we shouldn't expect them to make and serve the teas and we certainly shouldn't ask them to live through lengthy and sad post mortems of our matches afterwards. Above all, by good-naturedly enabling us to continue playing the sport deep into the twilight of our careers, we were not to infer that they actually liked the game.

The passing years changed things, too, and continue to do so. Many cricketers forget that the achingly gorgeous girl-friend who accompanied them to matches in their twenties has evolved, still achingly gorgeous of course, quarter of a century later into someone with different priorities. She marches to the rhythm of a sterner drum these days, and the lure of an afternoon on the boundary's edge, attractive as that may well continue to be, is replaced by the reality of looking after children and generally getting stuff done. For the cricketer to be cross about this is ridiculous. He should just be cringingly grateful that she is happy to do this, thus allowing him to go on playing, and his local florist should be able to declare a dividend many times over on the strength of his appropriately expressed gratitude. If, from time to time, he is prevented from playing a match by the realities of domestic chores or family parties, he should accept with good humour.

'One of the most beautiful qualities of true friendship,' said Seneca, 'is to understand and be understood'. The tragedy for most not very good male cricketers is that the agony is bound to go on for much longer than the match itself, as they will be returning home to someone who does not really understand cricket, and does not really want to, either. If you get mugged, you can go home and receive support and sympathy. Ditto if you crash your car. Ditto if you discover that Vladimir Putin is your third cousin. But if you take a heroic blinder at second slip off the Yacht Designer's 'arm ball', and follow that up by bludgeoning the winning runs, you must feast on the memory alone and in private. The last time I scored a 50, I was determined not to mention it when I got home, choosing instead the more glorious route of having the information prised out of me by a spell-bound family, who would then be truly impressed. It didn't work. No matter how many leads and hints I gave them, they simply didn't ask. Finally, I had to proffer the information myself ('guess how many runs Dad made today?') in a pathetic attempt to make sure they all knew. One of them looked up from a copy of Asterix in Switzerland and muttered absent-mindedly: 'Oh. that was good. What's a fondue?' Actually, it wasn't even 50; it was 35. Or 19. I forget which.

So, just as there are no more than seven stories in the literary world, so there are only four girls in White Hunter cricket.

It is a Saturday in August, and there are four girls sitting on a long garden bench by the scoreboard, each apparently watching the proceedings with sceptical attention. None of them exists, of course, but each one has been invited along as a stereotype, a stereotype being quite the best thing to be invited along to a cricket match as. They arrived here by different routes, physically and metaphorically, and it is a fair bet that most would not actually have chosen to be here if all else was equal. The trouble is, all things are definitively not equal. If Anton Chekov were alive today, he would produce an entire four act play based on the things they said to each other on that bench, and on the pregnant silences in between. They are wrapped up against the elements, and there is a communal rug stretching just about across the four of them, which reminds us again of the most intractable of their problems, the weather.

The first girl under the rug turns up once a year, normally because there happen to be two nearby gardens open for the National Garden Scheme. When she arrives, which tends to be just as tea is being cleared away, she is delighted to be among old friends, and very marginally aware of the game in progress somewhere behind her. She reads the Gardening section of the Sunday papers until someone points out that her other half is bowling, when she has the appearance of needing to be told what bowling is, or what it does. She claps enthusiastically when he gets hit for three consecutive fours, as that is what quite a few of the spectators are also doing, and she says 'Oh Dear!' with sympathy when he finally buys a wicket off the last ball of his final over. 'Was that good, what you did?' she asks innocently when he comes back in, and then goes inside to help wash up the tea. A cricket match for her is like an annual First Aid refresher course for anyone else, in that you wouldn't really choose to do that sort of thing with your time, but you never quite know when you will need the knowledge again. Let us call her the Garden Designer.

The second girl is a master of the universe, or rather a very senior fund manager in a very senior investment company. She earns more than all the other White Hunters put together, but the only way you can tell this is by the marginally smarter jeans she is wearing than everyone else. She reads the Business Section of the papers, and turns each page as if she is expecting to find herself overleaf, which she normally does. The Financial Adviser is in awe of her, mainly because he has never met anyone in the White Hunters who has enough money to actually need his advice. She exudes a steely bull-market expectation that her husband will come up to scratch when he goes out to bat, and a bearish sense of the inevitable when he trawls back in to the pavilion three minutes later because he has been run out by a twelve year old Spanish boy with a slight limp. You might very well think that something this frivolous would irk a captain of industry, or at least pass serenely under her radar, but you would be wrong. It's that old mental green belt thing again, and even the dire fielding exploits of the Grenadier strengthens her in some way for the coming week of achievement.

The third girl is cross, and has been ever since she got up. She is only at the match because, besides her husband, one of her children is playing, and because her car broke down outside Waitrose the previous evening, and she mistakenly thought that even a cricket match would be better than staying at home. Cricket, to her, panders to all the worst things in men- their vanity, their frivolity and the comfort that they find from being in a state of drift. Men who would appear to her meaningful and interesting round the dinner table, for example, are transformed into giggling idiots by the mere fact of having dressed in off-white or gripping a bit of willow. She looks up from the Review section of the Sunday paper and asks resignedly how long 35 overs will last. Unimpressed with the answer, she works on a futile attempt at solving 3 down in the cryptic crossword: 'Member slides back on field. (3,4)'

Ironically, the final girl under the rug simply can't get enough of cricket, and she will be found at every match of the season. Where others see a chewed-up cricket pitch, she sees only beauty; where they see pathetic middle-aged men pulling non-existent muscles, she sees only heroes. She even rushes her morning chores to ensure that she can be at the match from start to finish. She will take over the scoring if anyone asks her to, and do it beautifully with different coloured pens to record the exploits of each batsman and bowler. She reads the main News section of the paper, partly because she has a vague interest in the news, but mainly because that was the only section left when she came to sit down. Either way, it doesn't really matter as she is much more intrigued by what is going on in front of her than she is by the fact of a Cabinet Minister being found making up to an ostrich on Clapham Common. She is quick to help chat up the members of a tricky opposition, and slow to pass judgement on the IT Man when he finds he can't lay his bat on a ball. The art of watching cricket was invented for her and she, in turn, was invented to make cricketers feel good about themselves.

We had one of these once. If anyone sees her, please can we have her back.

Chapter 12

THE SHOCKERS

Forgive your enemies, but never forget their names
John F Kennedy

The dream doesn't always work out.

It begins with a genial conversation. A winter walk takes place on the South Downs Way. The talk idly turns to cricket. Someone gives someone else a business card in the pub afterwards. The first someone plays for an occasional team up on the Surrey border. 'We're always on the look-out for new oppositions,' they say. 'You should talk to our fixtures secretary'. We do, and he is charming. He refers us to the club website which habit forbids us from visiting. This is a mistake as it turns out, as everything we would need to know to make a sensible judgement is there on the Home Page. He confirms that they have, indeed, got a gap, and would be delighted to come down to us and play a Sunday fixture. In five months' time, we will discover exactly why they have regular gaps in their fixture list, and why we will be ensuring they have another one this time next year. However, for now all we know is that we are scheduled to play The Surrey Shockers at home in early July, and another brick has been cemented into the wall of the upcoming season.

A few weeks before the match, contact is made with the Shocker's skipper, and the first tiny doubts seep in. He is called Mike, and he is put out that you called him at work. He is efficient, clinical and curt, all of which happen to be characteristics that the White Hunters have tried unsuccessfully to learn over the years. We tend to be inefficient, vague and long-winded. All he wants from you is the post code of the pitch, and a confirmed start time. You tell him both of these, and add that The White Hunters normally forgather at the Hinton Arms for a swift couple before the game. He sniffs and says he doubts anyone will have time to do that, but thank you anyway. Deflated, you go back to the day job, executing a perfect imaginary square cut with the phone on your way back to the kettle.

On the Sunday in question, an advance guard of Hunters leaves the pub after a mere two pints just in case any of the visitors have arrived early. A line of dark executive cars indicates that they all have. Half of them seem to be concluding business deals on smart phones, whilst the others are manhandling huge coffins of personal kit to the front of the pavilion. Many are young, crop-haired and worryingly tall. 'Where's the changing rooms?', one of them asks. 'We normally change in that shed', The Tree Hugger volunteers, and points at an old gang mower and a small heap of broken bats. The silence is ominous.

By the time the remaining Hunters have arrived at the pitch, what looks like a full scale game of cricket is taking place among the younger Shockers. Balls are hurled across the outfield from fielder to keeper, lobbed to the batsman who fires impossible catches back at the fielders, who pouch them with ease. The HR Manager tries to join in by mistake, as he is easily confused, and they just stare at him.

At the toss, which is with Carl, because Mike can't be bothered to captain the side in unimportant matches, The Tree Hugger makes the suggestion we always make when a new team arrives:

'Thirty five overs a side. Maximum of 6 overs a bowler. Retire at 50. Avoid LBWs unless they are back-leg, middle stump plum. Oh, and we have a tradition of playing not out first ball. OK?'

Carl looks at him as if he has just appeared on the sex

offender's register.

'Sorry, mate. We always play declaration games. Would have thought that Mike would have explained that. 20 Overs after 6.00pm. And we don't retire batsmen. Ever. And there are no limits to the number of overs we bowl. And I think our guys know how to adjudicate an LBW, but thank you anyway. But apart from that, perfect'.

The Tree Hugger, always a more convincing host than negotiator, agrees to this for the sake of a quiet life, but holds out for the not out first ball rule. Carl wins the toss, and says that we can have 'first dig', a new and unfamiliar expression on The Tree Hugger, who consequently isn't sure if we are batting or bowling when he comes back to his friends afterwards. He doesn't like to ask, as he feels that this demonstration of ignorance will only make things worse. He spots the Shockers heading on to the outfield, works out that we are batting, and decides that, for old time's sake, he and I will open the innings.

The Private Client, who is our best batsman and habitual number 3, is running late on the A34 half way between Oxford and Newbury and his phone has run out of battery. His phone has always run out of battery because, besides knowing everything there is to know about global commodity markets, The Private Client knows the square root of nothing about getting somewhere on time. We have more chance of happening upon a Higgs boson particle buttering the sandwiches than of seeing The Private Client before the toss.

We bat OK, in the event, as we often do if we feel unappreciated by the opposition. There is something in hostility that stiffens the sinews and makes even the most fragile batsman determined not to give his wicket away. Even The Human Sieve can be relied upon to go at least three shots without executing the traditional waft outside the off-stump. It strikes some of us that, as a team, we would have achieved so very much more in the last 25 years if we had stuck to playing dislikeable teams.

I tend to club anything on or around middle stump past or above square leg, whilst missing most things wide of the wicket. The Tree Hugger sticks his tongue half way down his chin and mutters 'concentrate … concentrate … concentrate' like a cross between a dealer in essential oils and Alastair Cook. He also picks anything off his middle stump and whacks it over mid-off, and makes a complete pig's breakfast of anything hittable. Both ironically profit from the pinpoint accurate bowling. Neither of us are pretty players, a phenomenon that leads the Shockers' obese and chippy keeper to make a litany of uncalled for remarks regarding their ancestry, background and prospects.

The Author top-edges a huge 6 over fine leg, and the bowler comes down to within 2 metres and glares at him, pulling his fingers across his throat in a foretaste of what might be about to happen. I have seen this all before, and I smile tepidly, more interested for the moment in the dawning realisation that The Tree Hugger could pass as a dead-ringer for Fred Goodwin, than I am in the imbecile glaring at me from just down the pitch. The pair put on 50 runs together, which is just as well as The Private Client has had to make a detour home, having failed to pack his cricket things before going out to his drinks party. He is still an hour from the pitch, and the urn has just been put on for tea.

Meanwhile, a rash of nicknames breaks out in the opposition camp. 'Jonno'. 'Bazzer'. 'Quackers'. 'Matty-boy'. 'The Stud'. The list goes on. For some reason, the White Hunters seem to prefer their nicknames with a frisson of subtlety, and it can put us off our stride when football-style ones appear on the pitch. 'Why', you sometimes find yourself asking the short square leg fielder, 'are you called the Nobster?' Actually, don't answer. I've just worked it out.

The second incident comes half way through the innings, when the bowler concerned deliberately runs into The Major, who is embarking on something as close to a quick single as a man can at a certain age and possessing a certain girth. This is a mistake for lots of reasons, one of which revolves around The Major's high centre of gravity. The Major has the dexterity and spatial awareness of an Emperor Penguin, which means that this kind of collision is just part and parcel of the charm of playing cricket with him. He has also been through much in life, and he has a relatively short fuse combined with a relatively broad vocabulary. He employs both, using his bat for emphasis, but no more. The bowler goes through a boring, macho routine involving expressions that most of us forgot at primary school, coupled with lots of middle finger pointing. The Major stares at him, smart enough to avoid escalation, but proud enough to want an apology.

All ghastly teams have a peacemaker. They have to have one, otherwise the team would cease to exist after a couple of seasons. In the case of the Surrey Shockers, the peacemaker looks like Andy Flower with a beard, and he wanders over to the square to calm things down. This is something he has done many times before, and he has an easy and practised air about him. He addresses them both as 'Gentlemen' which, whilst being only 50% accurate, is 100% effective. The Major returns to his crease, the Bowler to his mark and The Groundsman to make a mental note never to let this team back to the ground again.

Tea consists of sandwiches, cakes, flapjacks and two incidents, one of which arises as a direct result of the other. Towards the end of the break, The Tree Hugger approaches Carl to let him know that the match fee is £100 for the team. Given that this includes 5 hours and 70 overs on one of the most beautiful pitches in England, and tea that could fell an elephant, £9.09 per head doesn't strike us as extortion. After all, the costs are real enough to us. However, it has the opposite effect on the Shockers.

'No, mate,' says Carl. 'We never pay for away games. It's free for us when we come to you, and free for you when you come back to us again next year. 'Simples,' he says, as he finishes with an annoying meerkat imitation.

The Hunters have this arrangement with a number of teams, but it relies on a number of factors, of which the most important is having some intention of actually organising a return match, something that has been off today's agenda since approximately 2.01pm. The team consensus is that if we never see this group of cricketers again it will be too soon, so there is rather more chance of Argentina giving up their claim to the Falklands than there is of us going travelling North to play them next season. It also helps if the visitors make any financial arrangement before the match, rather than during it. However, we concede the point, as we play this game for enjoyment, not as an expression of machismo. It will cost club funds 70% of what is left in the bank account, but it is worth it just to avoid real unpleasantness. Equally, we also decide that we will extend our innings 2 overs after the tea break, just to make the slightly childish point that we are not a complete push-over. This leads more or less immediately to Incident number 3.

Two angry bowlers short-pitch the next 12 balls at the heads of The Poet and The Sieve, possibly the two worst batsmen in The Northern Hemisphere. As well as being dangerous, it is entirely counter-productive, as The Sieve is far too short to be troubled by short bowling and The Poet is located far too far East of the leg stump to be inconvenienced either. Both are relatively unperturbed until the penultimate ball, where The Poet waves a bat at the passing missile, gets a thick touch which loops over slip and to deep third man for 4, after which he solemnly raises his bat to his adoring lurcher on the boundary's edge. Sometimes, poetry can be wordless.

Sometimes, too, beauty can be wasted. How many hours have we sat with one of our cherished regular oppositions, and watched the rain pouring down onto an already sodden square? How many times have we had to cancel matches that we have all been thoroughly looking forward to? Why is it that today of all days, when a large dump of snow would be entirely welcome, the conditions at our home ground are at their breathless best. Unbroken sunshine spotlights the emerald of the outfield , the parched strip and the shadows beneath the ash trees away to the North. The Magistrate's geraniums have never been so red, picked out against the dark Cedars of Lebanon in the grounds of the nearby college. No rain is forecast for decades, and it won't get dark until at least 3 hours after we have finished the game. Pigeons and buzzards coo and mew respectively and just about everything is fine with the world. Just about.

When the Shockers start their innings, Batsman 1 is blond

and huge, and does an Alec Stewart sort of things with his legs on the way to the wicket, kicking them up behind him like a Viennese dressage horse. Or maybe that was Robin Smith. He is from Down Under, and parades the chip on his shoulder like a dachshund being taken for a walk in Hyde Park. He attacks the crease as if he has a civil engineering project in mind, and The Groundsman winces at deep square leg. He takes guard by shouting 'two' up the pitch and looks around. What he sees both disappoints and encourages him.

He sees The Poet opening a can of Guinness on the boundary's edge, and placing it in the crook of a tree for future consumption. He sees The Private Client racing up the track in a cloud of dust, still dressed as for the drinks party he has recently left. He sees The HR Manager, The Accountant and The Investor animatedly discussing a film they saw last week. He sees The Land Agent walking towards The Groundsman's house to deliver a small pot of marmalade. He sees The Financial Adviser lighting a small cheroot at second slip, and The Major donning a surgical support at Fine Leg. He sees The Sieve optimistically stretching, and The Tree Hugger and I looking depressed.

The umpire calls 'Play', but we discover that no one has brought out a match ball, so another delay ensues. The Sieve tries fruitlessly to engage Batsman 1 in conversation, gives up, and tells an entirely unfunny story about Nando's to The Financial Adviser.

Having spent all morning making the tea, The Magistrate is clearing it up, and inadvertently walks behind The Land Agent's run-up before he has even bowled the first ball. Batsman 1 backs away and holds his hand up:

'Somebody tell that woman to get out of the way,' he says. No one reacts, but the air is alive with the faint sound of straws breaking camels' backs and final nails being inserted into coffins.

The eventual first ball is straight enough, and Batsman 1 comes forward, blocking it with exaggerated defence and shouting 'Wait on, Timmy!' very loudly at Batsman 2. He does the same with the second ball, even though The Private Client misfields it. The third ball is very wide but, before the umpire can stretch his arms out, The Land Agent good-humouredly holds them in against his body so he can't. The gesture is misinterpreted, which at least places The Land Agent in familiar territory. Thus it is that the Shockers bat very slowly, very sensibly and very tediously. So slowly, sensibly and tediously do they bat, that even the less astute White Hunters begin to realise that something is up. They may be a poisonous team, but they are good cricketers, and, as such, should be getting amongst us from early in the piece.

What is up is that the Surrey Shockers have also decided to make a point. And the point they have decided to make is that they will go for a draw from the very start, and will theatrically block out every ball bowled to them for the next couple of hours. They will do so because they are cross that we have batted on for two overs after tea, even though they have a minimum of 40 overs to score 219 runs, not exactly out of their reach. And they will do so because, whatever else they do and know and feel, they do not understand cricket in any sense of the term that we understand it. It turns out that they truly believe that a good way to end their day out in the country is to drive the 30 or so miles back up the A3 having made their point, rather than having had a good match, or thrashed us, or been narrowly beaten, or had a pint with us, or anything else.

At a stage in a game like this, cricket becomes a Kafkaesque piece of farce, consisting of two completely unrelated activities taking place on the same stage. Both activities are called cricket, but they have less to do with each other than Tony Blair had to do with Newcastle United Football Club. Meaning nothing.

Tree Hugger puts The Author on, as nothing so accelerates scoring opportunities as his gentle brand of slow leg side full tosses. Each one is studiously blocked out, and he bowls a maiden over, the first he has ever bowled in 668 overs of trying. The Tree Hugger bowls at the other end. Same result. Even the Sieve takes off his pads and bowls an over. It goes for 6, which is coincidentally the number of wides he has bowled before he completes the task. The Investor says 'Oh, for fuck's sake' and Batsman 1 glares at him. We have no option but to try to get them out, so the joke bowlers come off, and The Investor and The HR Manager come on.

Wickets fall from time to time, but the result is a foregone conclusion. 33 overs later, with the Shockers on 85 for 5, 124 short of our total. Most of these runs have resulted from extras, or from a single batsman who ignored the instruction not to score runs. Both skippers shake hands and agree to put the match out of its misery. The Groundsman, for whom great animation is normally expressed in no more than the slight raising of one eyebrow, strides in from square leg and wrenches the stumps out of the ground. Maybe they just didn't know that he had taken the afternoon off work on Thursday to prepare the pitch for them, that he had been mowing the square at 9 the previous evening, that he had been out as soon as the dew was dry that morning to paint the lines. Maybe.

A manner of détente is maintained after the match, during which Mike formally invites us back to their home ground the next summer. Our response is enigmatic, but it dawns on us later that the Shockers have really enjoyed their day out in the country, and rather appreciated us as a team. They evidently don't get out enough, unlike The Sieve, who gets out all the time. 'Small penises,' said The Financial Adviser philosophically. 'Big egos'.

Long after their executive convoy had headed back up the

track towards the leaded lights of South West Surrey, a few of us sat in the Hinton Arms and reflected on it all.

The Poet parked a Guinness and a round of chicken sandwiches in front of himself and leaned back in his chair.

'Do you know?', he said. 'I actually rather enjoyed today.' Various people expressed curiosity at this. 'No, really,' he went on, draining the dregs of the evening's inaugural pint. 'Not only is it the longest innings I have ever had against anyone, but it's all made me realise just how brilliant 95% of our cricket actually is. I had begun to forget how precious each one of these days is after a certain age. Now I know.'

It was an unorthodox view, but somehow we knew he was right. Sometimes in life you need to go to the dentist to appreciate just how good a morning is when you don't.

He looked around for a reaction and then down at the lurcher, who was too busy polishing off the last of his chicken sandwiches to meet his gaze.

Chapter 13

ONE SATURDAY IN AUGUST

'For every mountain there is a miracle'
Robert H Schuller

Ever since the cosmic demotion of humankind started in earnest five hundred years ago with Galileo and others pointing out that we may not be on our own in the universe, man has futilely tried to convince his wife he needs Saturday afternoon off for sport. This need is often dismissed as selfish or, worse still, childish. It is, in fact, the primeval assertion of his demanding role as Alpha Male and Hunter-Gatherer rolled into one. Sport has become the only avenue where he can express the link with his pre-historical heritage, short of total war or – in extremis

– membership of the Conservative Party. And, since he is so busy hunting and gathering from Monday to Friday, he is restricted to weekends and occasional Wednesday evenings.

It is a Friday evening in August, the month after we played the Shockers, and we have a match the following day. I am mowing the lawn, as I will need to spend a good deal of Saturday morning trying to avoid phone calls from players who have forgotten to tell their wives that they have a match, and are exploring the possibilities of bailing out. Of course, they never actually say that they have forgotten. They are far more imaginative than that. The way they put it, their wife is almost begging them to go off and fulfil their cricketing duties and, but for this tiny but hugely urgent matter that has just come up, would have almost certainly come along, too.

Until I started to run a roving team, I had no notion just how many pets die every day in the UK, and how many of them are seemingly connected to our players. Equally, I was unaware just how many urgent work and school matters arise over the breakfast table on Saturday morning, and require sorting before nightfall. To be fair, it has all given me a glimpse of a Britain I had no idea existed.

Twenty years have passed since Bolton Abbey, and today we have a home match. This brings joy and worry in equal measure. Joy because the ground is lovely, and so are The

Groundsman and The Magistrate. Worry, because we live in a temperate maritime climate, where rain is frequent and where the clay-cap on which we play our cricket has all the porosity of a galvanised dustbin lid. The ducks that The Human Sieve regularly provides us with are not alone on the ground once an area of low pressure settles over Ireland. Even an ostrich would have to borrow some water wings if it fancied walking over to inspect a length. Weather plays an unavoidably big part in a cricket organiser's life, and not just for the obvious reasons. Our matches punctuate every summer's progress like the pings on an ECG chart, so the prevailing weather conditions for each match are what you group together to remember over the next few years. In 2009, we were defeated by rain almost as often as by our opponents, and therefore I assume it was a wet and miserable summer. In 2010, on the other hand, we didn't lose one minute's play to the elements, meaning that it was probably long and delightful. In reality, both were thoroughly average, and we just happened to end up luckier in one than in the other. Years ago, a rained off match would be the cue for a visit to the Go-Kart track en masse, or to some unsuitable film. Nowadays, we all tend to troop off meekly home and volunteer for jobs that we have spent weeks negotiating our ways out of. But yesterday's rain disappeared in the night, and BBC Southern Counties have forecast hours of warm sunshine for today. That means The Groundsman will be busy marking out the lines, instead of staring balefully out to the build-up of clouds in the West and wondering when to make the cancellation call.

We have always found that a call to the opposition skipper pays dividends on the morning of a match day. This is not to remind him of the fixture – or at least hopefully not – or even to tell him how to get to the ground. It is to assess his general state of morale, and to gauge whether or not he has a full compliment of players. If he has ten, and we have twelve, then it is the work of a moment to provide him with someone truly bad, suitably repackaged as raw talent, by way of a gift. This at once establishes moral superiority while it still has enough time to seep into his thinking, and it also makes him worry slightly that maybe, just maybe, the Hunters have turned a corner. We haven't, but it doesn't matter. The White Hunter road of mediocrity has fewer corners on it than Route 66.

Actually, this mediocrity is, in management-consultant speak, vertically integrated. Meaning that the four cricketing institutions that I would like to do well (me, the White Hunters, Sussex and England) are all prone to endless bouts of awfulness. I have tried many times to transfer my allegiances elsewhere, but it doesn't work. Whole books have been written on the reason why this should be. Today, as it happens, all four are playing, which should make for good coverage in tomorrow's sports pages. England have recently let everyone down by winning the Ashes for the first time since the Black Death, and Sussex, having imported, in Mushtaq Ahmed, their first really good player in 168 years of trying, counter-intuitively won the County Championship in 2003, 2006 and 2007. Therefore, for the time being it is only the White Hunters and me flying the flag of under-achievement.

The visiting team, a cheerful village side from East Sussex, are playing us for the first time. This makes peripheral activities like the toss more important than ever. The trick is to bring along an old cricket ball and bounce it knowingly on the wicket, commenting to the opposing skipper that 'we got some lateral movement off it' last weekend, 'it spun like a top for The Yacht Designer'. Even though we don't really understand what 'lateral movement' is, and even though The Yacht Designer has never spun a ball in his life, the seeds of doubt have already been sown.

The Investor joins me for the toss. We sometimes do this, as we find strength in numbers, and someone else to share the blame with when it all goes wrong. Also The Investor is someone who will have to do more that his fair share of batting and bowling, so he might as well have a say in the outcome. He does everything with elegance, The Investor, and manages to look calm and in some sort of control even when he is actually not on speaking terms with his bat, or the ball. The Investor is charming, and he came to us well into our second decade, riding in on the breeze one day like a male Mary Poppins. He does something to do with money, which makes those of us who don't have anything to do with money rather impressed. He is also one of those tragic middle-aged men who punish themselves on a bike, and in lycra, throughout the summer, which means that he is often crocked. But for now, he also has many home games under his belt, and so has a good idea of how the pitch is going to behave.

The trick with the toss itself is not to win it. That way, the decision you might have made will never be criticised by your team-mates, and you may avoid being blamed for the loss of the game. In the unfortunate event of winning the toss when captain, though, the aim is to contrive to look pleased and to avoid panic. For this reason, I find that it is important to have canvassed opinion among colleagues before going out into the middle, so that I have a reasonable idea of what I will do if I actually do win the toss. It avoids embarrassing delays. If it has rained in the last 24 hours, I tend to insert the visitors, on the basis someone once told me that things should speed up as it dries out. If it is forecast to rain half way through the afternoon, I tend to bat as, let's face it, we would all rather bat than bowl if we could only do one of them. If all else fails, state confidently that 'we prefer chasing' and go back to face the wrath of The Farmer.

Today, we lose the toss and are asked to bat. So far, so good.

Then the nightmare of the batting order. Messrs Flower and Strauss have it easy in this respect. They seldom have to worry about who didn't get a go last time, who got a shocker of a decision at Adlestrop, or who should bat down the order as they're likely to get a good bowl, and it wouldn't be fair to put them higher than 6. You can also bet that they don't usually have a player on the field who none of them have ever seen with a bat in his hands.

The general rule is that no one wants to bat 1, 2, 9, 10 or 11. The jackpot is to bat at 4, 5 and 6, whilst most people would settle at a pinch for 3, 7 and 8. My tendency is start at the extremes and work inwards. Do little deals along the way ('I want to save you for a long spell today' etc) and remind players of past kindnesses, as you ask them 'to provide some backbone in the lower order'. It is a sign of weakness, though none the worse for that, to fill in the first five places and then indicate that you will see how things develop before completing it. Filling in the number 10 and 11 slot is made much easier if you have late-comers in the team, as they have made the metaphorical bed they now have to lie on. However, it's also an inconvenient truth that our habitual late-comer happens to be The Private Client, who also happens to be our most consistent batsman once the effect of his liquid lunch has worn off.

It's also sometimes more handy than you might think to have someone who has never played the game before on the books for each match. They are unlikely to complain when they get pencilled in to the number 11 spot; they might not be able to play cricket, but they can play a vital role in helping a skipper avoid unpleasantness. Equally, as the organiser, ensure you save a comfortable berth for yourself: you'll be happy that you did, and your team will respect you not a shred more if you don't. After all, I very much doubt that Napoleon made himself back marker on the Retreat from Moscow.

Finally, ignore ringers. When that sturdy friend of a friend in the faded MCC sweater who 'does a bit of everything' presents himself, the chances of him being other than useless are roughly zero. New White Hunter players have always tended to contribute in inverse proportion to the amount of build-up they have been given in the days leading up to the match. Usually, it is the university blue who tells us that he opened for his college only a few years back, but who fails to tell us that it was in the cross-country trampoline, or poetry declamation. Besides, all our players started life in the White Hunters as supposed ringers, didn't they?

Twenty years on, the cast list has changed somewhat, talent constantly leaking in and out of the side by some mystical process of osmosis. Gone are The All-Rounder, The Timber Matting Contractor, and The Brand Builder. In their places came The Financial Adviser, The Private Client, The Walking Duck and even The Human Sieve.

Today, The Yacht Designer and The Human Sieve will open the batting, so it will be prudent for 3 and 4 to be padded up and ready. Number 5 would be advised not to stray too far from his bat, either.

And so, on three separate grounds in England, Andrew Strauss takes guard to face Ben Hilfenhaus at Lords, Ian Westwood prepares to face Yassir Arafat at Edgbaston, and The Human Sieve settles in his crease to face Jim Someone or Other for the first ball of the day, somewhere in a wooded bit of Hampshire. The Sieve exudes confidence this July afternoon, and for a ball or so, one can dimly see why. The sun is shining, birds are singing and a man is umpiring who wouldn't know what an LBW shout was if it jumped up and bit him on the arse. The Sieve executes his trademark slash over second slip to third man and is off the mark with a single, coincidentally reaching his season's best score in the process.

The Yacht Designer gets served up three rank long hops. He lathers the first two to the square leg boundary and the third into the face of the short square fielder, compressing the broken frame of his glasses into the bridge of his nose, and stunning him into a moaning heap of red and white on the ground. Some enthusiast brings out the team defibrillator, just on the off-chance that he is having a heart attack and the machine can get its first use. To the enthusiast's evident disappointment, he isn't. The Groundsman brings out a towel, though more to keep the blood off his square than for any medical reason. A consensus is reached that the man needs to go to A and E to have his nose reconstructed. (Five hours later his colleagues realise with horror that he is still there, as no one thought to pick him up after he had been repaired, and he hadn't got a mobile phone to remind them).

The batsmen crossed during the incident, so The Sieve is facing again. Another trademark slash, this time better directed, brings him two runs and his highest score for three seasons. Then the brush with excellence is all too much for him, and he is clean bowled next ball attempting a parody of the Dilshan Scoop.

After one over, we are 12-1, and the opposition are down to ten men. The Sieve is replaced by The Private Client, who has had to be cut out of the wreckage of his own hangover to ply his trade in the middle. He starts slowly, with the air of a man remorselessly scanning the horizon for a spare paracetamol, but then begins to connect, and adds an increasingly cheerful 50 runs with The Yacht Designer. He then puts on another cheerful 50 with The Financial Adviser's son, and the Hunters are unusually poised at 122-3. There is always a danger point in each match where the gremlins get amongst us, and we begin to self-destruct after a reasonable start. We get bored, possibly, or we become scared of heights all of a sudden, terrified of what we would actually do with a score that had a '2' in front of it. It is this that we now have to avoid.

It's my turn now, complete with my sense of determinism that dictates that I have no control whatsoever on what will unfold, and that fate already knows not only what I will score, but how I will be out. I have noticed that this philosophy applies to many Hunters, which makes the long evenings in the nets during the Springtime rather hard to understand and even harder to justify. In the event, I get 10 in four scoring shots, and am clean bowled by someone with a beard. 132-4. Tree-Hugger is clean bowled by someone without a beard, but not before he has hit 14. 152-5. The Financial Adviser is out for a second ball 6, caught in the deep by a bloke with spots, off the bowling of the man without a beard. 156-6. The Investor, who is all feints, dabs and nurdles, oils his way to 14, but the Land Agent carves an almighty second ball yahoo straight into the grateful fingers of the brother of the man with spots, at long on. 175-8. The IT Man muddles to 2, leaving The Groundsman to tip us over the 185 run barrier in our 35 allotted overs. The man without a beard ends up with 3 wickets, but still doesn't remember his friend in the Winchester A and E.

If The Financial Advisor's body is a temple, which it may well be, it is a temple built along the generous lines of The Parthenon or Ankor Wat. Substantial, historic and comforting. However, right now it is a temple moving at speed towards the Victoria Sponge, and it becomes the starting gun for the best moment of any cricketer's day – the match tea. Up at Lords, Andrew Strauss is on 135 not out, which might be pretty enjoyable in itself (I wouldn't know), but you can still detect his pace quickening when he runs up the pavilion steps at 3.40 for his cuppa. For all I know, he may well harbour some nightmare fear that The Financial Adviser has levered himself over the Lords railings, climbed into the ground and is even now tucking in to the chocolate brownies. Stranger things have happened.

Tea is the best moment to approach the opposition for a match fee, as it is probably the happiest they will be all day, and they will not yet want to blot their copybook before the second innings. It is also supposed to be a time of networking. Not professional networking, which would be pitiful and anyway, most people don't need a yacht designed for them these days, but recruiting from the opposition's talent pool. Moreover, careless talk abounds about a return fixture the following July, an event that is made less than likely by the strange polarity that seemingly equips The White Hunters to travel West and North, but not East or South. Admittedly, if they travelled more than a handful of miles southwards, the opposition would have dorsal fins.

Towards the end of tea, the more enthusiastic Hunters drift onto the outfield to play catch with a moth-eaten old ball that has been through the gang mower on at least five separate occasions. Traditionalists would call this fielding practice, a term that doesn't really do justice to the gentle arthritic lobs that are offered, and dropped, inside a small intimate circle of friends. Rather engagingly, each time they catch a ball, they look back at the pavilion to make sure that the opponents have noticed. It never occurs to them that they will have seen the drops as well.

The Human Sieve is padding up to keep wicket, and I am frantically trying to work out who to throw the new ball to. Again, this is not a problem with which Ricky Ponting is having to wrestle. He doesn't have to give Hilfenhaus first go just because he didn't get a bat, or because he had been kind enough to drive him to the ground. He puts him on first because that's what he wants to do. And I'll bet he never threw the ball to Glen McGrath just to shut him up. No wonder he won so many matches. I choose the teenager, on the basis that there will be a fit of angst if I don't choose him, and because he will probably have digested the brownies quicker than anyone else.

Up at Edgbaston, Warwickshire are making something of a comeback after a dire start. The Sussex skipper, Mike Yardy, is a man after my own heart. From the broad canvas of not being brilliantly good at cricket, he has gone on to play for England and captain his county. This he has done through a combination of grit, enthusiasm and lack of alternatives. There is something reassuringly British about the story of a man who, one winter, has to work in a sports shop at Gatwick Airport as no representative or overseas club side wants him on its books, and the next winter is part of the England one day team. The sport would be an altogether happier place if its world consisted of more Yardies and less Pietersons, as generosity of spirit still has something to do with it all. It may well be that, in this instance, he has decided to bring on his joke bowlers so as to make a game of it. After all, the team will have checked into their Birmingham hotel for four nights and they need to make the match last the distance.

At Lords, a match which England will eventually go on to win for the first time at 'Headquarters' since the builders of Stonehenge were applying for planning permission, England are gently subsiding from 196-0 to 425 all out. Again, I imagine that Strauss is keen not to risk batting Australia out of the game. Here in the Hampshire hills, normal service has been resumed. The opening bowlers serve up a series of long hops and delicious half volleys, and the Sussex village moves swiftly to 60-0 after 11 overs. The great thing about a teenager delivering self-service bowling is that, as with all other teenage matters, they react by sensing that the whole failure is part of some giant conspiracy concocted by their father with the help of the rest of the team. I take both openers off, and immediately things change.

The first ball bowled by The IT Man is pummelled toward long-on out of the meat by the bloke with a small beard. It travels so quick, and so straight, that the fielder concerned (me, since you ask) is faced with just one of two choices: get right out of the way, or get out of the way consistent with being seen to have made an effort to catch the thing. Among team-mates, option 2 tends to play better, so I stick a right hand up to roughly where the ball will pass, but I can't even get that right. When the ball eventually comes to rest in the palm of my hand, only I know that I was actually looking at the ground when it got there. I accept the applause modestly. 60-1. The very next ball, the batsmen having crossed, precisely the same thing happens with precisely the same result. 60-2.

This change of circumstance encourages me to give Tree-Hugger an over or two, normally the prelude to a much increased scoring rate. But the number 3 batsman is so grimly fascinated by the fact that Tree-Hugger's tongue sticks out during his run up, that he loses concentration and runs himself out. 62-3. In cases like this, it is quite wrong for the bowler not to be credited with the wicket. Tree-Hugger has spent decades getting this deformity right, and has taken many wickets with it. And on it all goes. The Investor bowls his spell of carefully thought out leg stump half volleys and persuades number 4 to spoon one down to where The Groundsman is dozing. 68-4. Aside from the small matter of the arrival at the crease of another, but much more convincing, Beard, we might actually win this one.

The new Beard does a number of things that worry a captain like me. He walks unsmilingly to the crease, for one, ignoring the routine pleasantries offered to him by The Sieve. He calls a curt 'Two please' to the umpire, and then glares at the field. The warning signs are everywhere. A faded club sweater. An equally faded hat. A rasta sweat band round each wrist. A preball routine. A bat with suspicious amounts of red round the sweet spot. A knowing glance at his partner. The businesslike air of a man who would prefer not to be there but, since he does not have that option, might as well settle things quickly. He puts the first ball he receives over the pavilion and immediately inspects his bat as if it hadn't performed correctly.

Short mid-off suddenly finds pressing business to attend to somewhere near the boundary. Volunteers for next change bowler vanish like hope in a nuclear winter.

Now, although The Beard and The Financial Adviser had never clapped eyes on each other in all their decades on the planet, it rapidly becomes apparent that they have somehow developed a visceral mutual loathing. Since every match needs spice, even a duel, I immediately add fuel to the fire by giving the next over to The Financial Adviser, whose competitive nature comes second to no one. Letting The Adviser bowl in this kind of situation is rather like adopting socialism – in that it is attractive enough in theory, but tends to be utterly barking in practise. The result is written in the stars anyway: the first ball sails over mid-on's head for a huge 6.

The Beard inspects his bat again with the suspicious air of a man who somehow felt it had just let him down for the second time, and proceeds to hit the next one even further. 104-4 and rising rapidly. The Financial Adviser cosmetically re-arranges the close fielders, in the humorous notion that they are likely to have anything whatsoever to do with the next few overs. He makes a sotto voce remark, just to rile The Beard, and fires a much quicker ball down outside the leg stump, which The Sieve waves politely past on its way to the boundary. 108-4. He then bowls an absolute snorter which goes right through the batsman, the keeper, and the five-bar gate on the boundary. 112-4.

A dog barks and the caravan moves on.

At the other end, The Land Agent and The Investor are keeping things under control, and starting to take the odd wicket. Even The Yacht Designer gets one to 'do something', apparently, and brings on a leading edge which he safely catches. To prove that I have learned something in all those years, I decide to forgo my own scheduled over and keep things as tight as possible. Or as tight as they could be in the context of the private battle between The Adviser and The Beard. I put on The IT Man, who keeps things quiet as well, once he has got over his sadness that I didn't put him on earlier, and didn't give him the nice end when I did. As he never tires of pointing out, form is temporary whilst class is permanent, which is, ironically, why he never got put on in the first place.

However, at 170-7, we have all but conceded the match. They have 4 overs and three wickets in hand to get another 16 runs. The man with spots gets a streaky four, and then a less streaky two. 176-7. Then he is cleaned up by The Land Agent, bringing in a man in thick glasses. Not thick enough, as it turns out, as he fails to see an inviting in-dip-per from The Financial Adviser, and departs second ball. 176-9. At the beginning of the penultimate over, The Beard is facing The Adviser with three wanted for a victory, and the latter obligingly serves up a long hop a foot outside the off-stump.

However, the two things a man should never do in life are to cut a spinner or pat a burning dog. In the absence of the latter, The Beard did the former, got a faint touch, which was gratefully pouched by The Human Sieve on the seventh attempt. The almost unbelievable entry in the score book read:

Beard: Caught Human Sieve. Bowled The Financial Adviser. 68

White Hunters won by 2 runs

There is, we concluded, a God after all.

Chapter 14

UNMANNERED YOUTH

'Youth is a wonderful thing. What a crime to waste it on children'
George Bernard Shaw

It is a little known fact that the Ten Commandments appear twice in the Bible, once in Exodus 34 and again in Deuteronomy 6. It is even less understood that Moses actually came down from Mount Sinai with three sets of stone tablets, not two, and that the third got lost in the mists of time. Maybe he fumbled it on the way down the mountain and dropped it. However, it is the contents of that third set of stone tablets which should divert us now.

For God was, and is, a recreational cricketer, and his views on behaviour on and off the pitch are every bit as strong as his views on worshiping golden idols, keeping the Sabbath or loving neighbours. More so, some think. For many boyhood years, God opened the batting alongside the Holy Ghost in my private games of Howzat, and it always surprised me how often the all-powerful deity would let himself fall LBW early in his innings, and not even refer it to the third umpire. The heavy run scoring somehow always tended to be done down at the bottom of the innings by Buddha and Mother Teresa, once the openers had blunted the bowling attack.

What the third set of stone tablets contained, according to Aramaic translations that have only recently come to light, was God's guidelines as to how children should behave on the cricket pitch, and how the parents of the said children should and should not conduct themselves. In a nutshell, they state that:

• Thou shalt not suffer a child to play in a match who cannot last through a 35 over innings without wanting to go back to the car and listen to Eminem.

• Thou shalt not, under any circumstances, alter an umpiring decision so as to let a distraught child continue an unattractive innings. Neither shalt thou deliberately drop a spooned-up catch offered by the said child.

• Thou shalt supply a helmet for everyone under the age of 18, for that is laid down in the MCC laws.

• Thou shalt not insert children into a close catching

position in front of the bat just because that's what Ian Bell does.

• Thou shalt not allocate an exalted batting position to a child who is completely useless, even be that child of thine own flesh and blood.

• But the greatest of all these commandments is this—that thou shalt not drag unseemly family squabbles onto the pitch, and so ruin everyone else's entertainment.

God eventually left my team to play in the Lancashire League, but his commandments live on, and, unlike their ten more illustrious companions, act as guidance for the White Hunters to this day.

Cricketers breed. They just do. And having bred, they have a habit at looking at their male children as being one small step away from the England Development Squad, even though they normally turn out to have as much talent for the sport as Shane Warne has modesty. This, ironically, makes them ideal candidates for the White Hunters.

The White Hunters have bred at least 100 replacements over the years, all without any artificial help from The Breeder himself. The oldest of these by now are soldiers, builders and merchant bankers, the youngest still mere babes in arms. Together they create an unstoppable, but entirely theoretical, well-spring of future talent and potential, most of it ultimately unrealised. This we jovially call our investment in the Club's future, before quietly returning to the side room that contains the hallucinogenic drugs.

Cricketing fatherhood is a multi-layered journey, marked out by how its different stages affect a man's ability to spend time in the middle, and his relationships with both offspring and wife. It pays to recognise these. It starts with pregnancy, when love is still very much in the air, and the blooming mother-to-be is at her most amenable to being persuaded to sit at a boundaries edge dispensing sandwiches and praise in equal measure. Co-operation like this will not appear again for 60 years, so enjoy it. Nor, in fact, will the sandwiches. At this stage, unless you have cheated and found out the child's sex earlier, you have an equal chance of having a girl (and thus potentially housing a real cricket world cup winner under your roof) as a boy (and thus just having someone who talks about it.).

It is at the toddling stage when things really get going. It is a time of innocence, of irony, and of contradiction. You, for example, will spend the tea interval lobbing soft balls at your child; he, in turn, will throw a hard bat at you when he tires of the experience. He will cry as you head in the middle to bat, whereas it will be you doing the crying when you return a couple of minutes later. No one on the ground admires you more than he does (apart, perhaps, from you), and long after others have run for the hills, he will be lapping up stories of your 1 for 87, or your catch at long leg. This is a joyful and rewarding time which, correctly handled, can set a man up for half a century of cricket.

The toddler gives way to the lad who, faster than you can know, becomes an adolescent. This is the pivotal moment when father and son find each other failing to live up to their ideals, or down to their prejudices. Communication is tricky at best, but equally, both quietly long for a shared enterprise that they can both do, and enjoy, together, without having to sacrifice strongly held positions, like those on pierced ears or gangsta rap. Cricket provides it. A day dawns when someone cries off, you have a gap in the team-sheet (see Preface), and, having rung around everyone in West Sussex and East Hampshire, you reach that moment of serenity when anyone will do. It is sufficient just to have 11 bodies on the pitch. The long wait is over. You are the proud possessor of a teenager, and the time has come for him to stride out into the middle, albeit in a pair of over-sized borrowed pads and a helmet that spent the winter full of jock straps and a half-eaten milk chocolate Bounty Bar.

The White Hunters do not have a youth policy, for to do so would have as much long term point as a Greek government bond. A youth policy would oblige the team to have an eye on the distant future, as opposed to the afternoon's sponge cake, which is as far ahead as most of us can see these days. It has to be said that, in spite of the general enthusiasm prevalent, a small minority of our younger players seem to remain blissfully unaware that they have just taken part in a cricket match until the opposition skipper says 'well done' to them at the end of the game.

The main point of bringing an embryonic cricketer to a match has, of course, little to do with the youngster, whose time will come in years to come. It is to complicate things for the opposition skipper. A sallow child in huge yellow pads and a smelly helmet acts as a tiresome qualification to his aim of blasting you off the pitch as soon as possible. Sportsmanship rears its ugly head, and he is captive to the general expectation that the lad will be given a sporting chance to do something. The most difficult thing to achieve as captain is the successful re-application of pressure once you have taken it off for a bit. When he goes out to bat, the youngster will find himself facing patronisingly gentle bowling, deliberately dropped catches and deliberately fluffed run-outs. The experienced adult cricketer will simply see this as an opportunity to profit from the confusion at the other end, and tuck into the friendly bowling and general bonhomie that abounds. Who knows, he might even get 20 or 30 runs before anyone notices.

Some of our junior cricketers are match-winners before their first shave. The Accountant's son disappeared for two years and came back as a 6'7" eighteen year old, taking five wickets for nothing in an evening match against a team that hadn't lost all summer. He even looked angry, which was perfect. The Financial Adviser's son had the ability of propelling a ball over the stumps from the deep mid-wicket boundary with a careless flick of the wrists, and running out elegant batsmen by half the length of the pitch. Others are more willing than able, and tend to turn up more for the underage beer and the banter than any particular love for the noble game. Some turn up once and flee for ever, but we have a handful of ten or so who find enough fascination in the whole thing to be reliably classed as part of the Club.

At the start of a game, the air is pregnant with psychological inter-generational challenges. First, the complex relationship between skipper and junior, particularly if the latter is a much better cricketer than the former, not an infrequent occurrence. There is a tightrope to be trod between being genial and patronising, and a second one between being decisive and dictatorial.

There is also the omni-present father to be considered, who will be lurking like a dark presence three yards south-east of short mid-on. He will either be determined that his son plays a brilliantly full part in the match, or won't actually be speaking to him. Either way, he will sidle up to you frequently and pressurise you. Equally, he will be completely useless himself, all talent supressed beneath the fictional weight of expectation he has put on himself and his son. If, as often happens, the skipper's own son is on the field, their complex power battles simply get re-located from home to the cricket pitch, all available for public inspection, and none the worse for that.

The Financial Adviser and Harry have led the way in all this for years. From every angle, they are opposites. One is tall and bowls fast; the other large and a spinner. One ranges the outfield like a caged tiger; the other drifts off to sleep at first slip, and strikes up conversations with neighbours who may be in need of some financial advice. Both are fine so long as the other is in a different county. Things normally start quietly, with no sign of friction. Then Harry will misfield, and The Financial Adviser will mutter 'Oh, for Fuck's sake'. Then The Financial Adviser will fumble a catch, and Harry will march all the way in from deep cover to make his extreme views known. When captaining a father and son unit of this nature, and both are good cricketers it should be said, we have developed the trick of offering them Number 1 and Number 11 in the batting order, but putting the onus on them to choose which. This has the effect of simultaneously making at least one of them happy, and making quite sure that there is no chance of them batting together.

Ironically, when father and son do actually bat together, it is normally the father who goes off-piste, and has to be dragged back towards his responsibilities by his son. By the same token, run outs are most likely to occur between this kind of pairing, often with venomous consequences during the next break of play.

The IT Man and Declan seemed to go many decades without actually talking. True, they would decant out of the same car at 1.45, and climb back in it 6 hours later, but that seemed to be the extent of their communication. Each would mock the other's efforts with the ball, and woe betide the team if they ended up batting together. If one dropped a catch, the other would travel 100 yards to ensure that everyone knew that the incident had not passed unappreciated. Then one season, everything had changed. Sweetness and light reigned, and honeyed compliments flew across the outfield like confetti. 'Well bowled, Dad!', says one. 'Not as good as yours', replies the other, and nine other cricketers head into the bushes to be sick. What had happened, we wondered? What had happened was explained by the arrival of a brand new personalised Mini at the next match, with Junior driving and the IT Man pillion. Expectation beforehand, and gratitude afterwards, had done the trick, as it so often does.

Nippers tend to want to open the batting, open the bowling and field in suicidally interesting positions close to the action. If their wish to open the batting gets granted, and they are any good, they tend to be back in the pavilion (clean bowled third ball for 8) before their partner has taken guard. When they aren't any good, and where we are playing a limited overs match in which we require 7 an over from the start, we find that they can be relied on to be holding up an end with the straightest of bats 12 overs later, having scored 3.

If they are given the new ball (and sometimes, after a big tea, they are the only people in the team physically capable of bowling) they try to be Malcolm Marshall and find that their first over has lasted 10 balls, and been hit for 16. The biggest contribution they can make is in fielding, where they can intercept, catch or chase down anything at all, without even breaking off conversation with the square leg umpire. Fielding, as every ageing cricketer knows, is the thing that starts to go first, and never looks back. The problem derives from the fact that, underneath it all we all care, and therefore we all try. Long after we should have given up trying, we still chase down balls at the boundaries edge, a potential cardiac event belied by the extreme lack of ground speed we actually achieve. The distance we can throw a ball declines by 2 metres a year until, one summer, someone gives up the pretence altogether, and rolls it in to the keeper underarm. The tragic sight of the sprinting Major being overtaken by a walking youngster on the Easton outfield in our disputed 2010 defeat, should probably have been enough to persuade most of us to pack it in.

Just occasionally, as has happened with The Accountant and his son (another Harry, as it happens), a form of capillary action removes talent from the father and pumps it into the son. The glad conclusion of this kind of process can be seen in the form of The Accountant smoking roll-ups by the pavilion whilst Harry wins matches for the club with the practised air of Meryl Streep collecting Oscars. This, it has to be said, is not something that is not likely to happen in my own family any time soon.

There are also moments of pure unexpected magic, which

is probably why we all still do it. Parents are allowed to want their children to do well, and cricket, by virtue of the sheer length and complexity of its games, gives plenty of opportunity. My younger son, Alex, played his first match for the Club in a needle fixture against the Kitchin Cabinet in Petersfield at the age of 12. He found himself not quite underneath a high, swirling, spinning catch at third man, massively top edged by a man we dearly wished to see the back of. As with his father, the co-ordination fairy had been sleeping on the job when Alex was born, so all 14 players on the pitch confidently expected the catch to be spilled. A small dog on the boundary's edge was readying itself to dash on and snatch the fallen ball, so confident was he in the eventual outcome. The bowler had returned half way to his mark in resigned expectation of bowling at the same batsman again. The umpire was looking at the stones in his hand and wondering why he could never remember how many more balls there were to be bowled during an over. Everyone was preparing to console and comfort, but against all probability, with arms outstretched first this way and then that, he clung on to ball by his fingertips. He looked at his hands, and at the faded red thing within them, with a look of incomprehension and disbelief, but that moment changed his life. The demons of low expectation began to give way to a measure of self-belief, because, having been held, that catch could never again be dropped. A school team wouldn't give an also-ran sportsman enough opportunity to gain that feeling, which is probably enough justification for the White

Hunters on its own. Monty Panesar knows what I am talking about.

There are other dynamics at work when father and son play cricket together, and every father should remember that one day his son will follow his example rather than his advice. When you find yourself the victim of a dubious LBW decision, for instance, and your son is batting at the other end, the inner conflict is palpable: the man in you knows that you should say 'well done' to the bowler, smile genially at the umpire, and then walk calmly off. The residual boy in you, who would be dominant were it not for the presence of your son, merely wants to explore just how far into the umpire's oesophagus a bat handle can go if correctly inserted. In the event, you tend to do a pathetic combination of the two, and your son is left having to pretend that this is the first time he has ever clapped eyes on you.

The first time my eldest son, Tom, ever heard me saying a truly bad word, really not a good word at all, was after I had been needlessly run out by the Financial Adviser at Great Durnford going for a third, just when I was showing signs of getting back into some sort of form after a long run drought. Three years later, he still manages to slip the incident into conversation should the subject of his language ever come up.

Some take their sport more seriously than others, and this can begin to interfere with their enjoyment. Compare and contrast, for example, Tom and Freddie. The latter is a talented late order batsman and off-break bowler of huge ambition but with a fragile youthful temperament. The former simply couldn't give a toss, having only turned up for the craich. One of the unfairnesses of sport is that Tom, on his day, can bludgeon 25 runs off a handful of lucky balls and return to the pavilion a happy man, whilst Freddie can be bitterly disappointed by a well-disciplined defensive innings of 10 that stretches over 7 overs. There is no answer to this. For it is just as likely that, when Freddie comes on to bowl a spell of immaculate in-dippers that same afternoon, he will be bowling at a man in prime form, who subsequently takes him to the cleaners. And when Tom gets a couple of overs, which he does simply because it was agreed between skippers that everyone would bowl at least one over, he takes three wickets all brilliantly caught on the long-on boundary from rank leg stump long hops. As with Tom, I have learned to restrict my ambition to hoping that one day, I will have the opportunity of facing myself bowling, much in the way that The Human Sieve longs to have a fellow kitchen gadget behind the stumps when he is batting.

Once a year, the August Bank Holiday Dads versus Lads match provides all the chances needed for settling domestic scores. The Land Agent, having begged to be given the bowling when his own two boys are out in the middle, goes for 30 runs off 3 overs. The Investor is bounced back into the pavilion by a son who has gone from 6 inches shorter than him to 6 inches taller in the time it took to eat the egg and cress sandwiches at tea. The times they are a'changing round here, and rather quicker than we thought they were. Few off us fare well but, as the sun begins to dip behind the hill we call home, I toss the ball to The Charity Worker for one last over at his 12 year old nephew. Only The Grenadier normally bowls worse, but he only went for 7 runs on his over today. The air is alive with promise, and I begin to wonder if today might not provide either of them with their first wicket in a quarter of a century of trying.

The Charity Worker beams and rotates his right arm in delight. He is not used to be asked to bowl, and he intends to make the most of it. The balls go very slowly, very high and reasonably straight, and the nephew is having trouble getting him off the square. And, when he does finally get a run, The Charity Worker intercepts him in mid pitch and gives him a huge bear-hug. He bowls well enough to be given another over, the last over of the match, as it happens. Again, it is better than anything he has served up in the last 25 years, and it only goes for 6 runs, one of which was a dropped catch. The general consensus, as we troop off for medals and bandaging, is that The Charity Worker has finally overcome the bowling gremlins, and should be allowed to bowl rather more overs in the coming season.

It doesn't happen. A few months later, deep into the close season, 20 or so White Hunters gather together at his memorial service. We talk about his defiant batting, his strange bowling and his awful running between the wickets. We talk about his resistance to our barracking, and about those bear hugs. We talk about all the memorable games we have played with him, and how much we loved him. And, in talking, we understand so deep down that the thought can hardly be defined, so strongly that it physically hurts, why we play this game, and why we want our children to play it, too.

Chapter 15

THE TRIUMPH OF THE SIEVE

'Cricket to us was more than play;
it was worship in the summer sun'
Edmund Blunden

The evenings draw in, and the team kit bag goes back to spend seven months in Tree-Hugger's garage.

Once the season is over, the different members of the team often won't see each other from September one year until April or May the next, even though they all live pretty close to each other. Over the years, it has turned out that this doesn't matter. We used to organise winter social events by way of applying some off-season continuation to the friendships that were forged during the summer. But to do so was sometimes to ignore the fact that a man can not only have many different friendships, but also different categories of friendship. Besides, you have to be quietly aware that there are others, others who may not have received your full attention during the frantic summer months, and who would quite like a bit more of it now. The key to a long and geriatric cricketing career is not to push your luck too far with your family during the off-season.

Whilst always pleased to see each other, we normally only plan to do so if cricket is in the air, and who knows or cares what the others get up to in the off-season? Actually, we do already know that The Yacht Designer goes to winter nets every week in the forlorn hope that he will eventually be blessed by the spin-fairy, and The Sieve nips into Specsavers just in case it is diagnosed that his eyes were the problem all along. They weren't.

The winters are long these days. It turns out that the Climate Change champions were either wrong, or exaggerating, or we were all missing the point. Snow lies thick on the ground now as it has not done for 50 years, and flooding rivers swirl around the low-lying towns and cities. Just at the point we all secretly thought that this unstoppable warming would allow us to play cricket when we never had before, January for example, a foot of snow falls on a length, and The Groundsman begins to wonder if it will be safe to let us back any time before midsummer's day. So we are left with nostalgia, that quiet ache that a dying season bequeaths to its bereaved. We lie in our beds as the rain lashes against the window and picture a moment, just one moment, from the previous season. And that one thought is enough to remind us why we do it, and why we will go on doing it until we don't even have the breath to call out 'No Ball!'

In the deepest mid-winter, the committee, which is really no more than a collective noun for anyone who fancies a drink on the evening in question, meets in the Three Horse-shoes at Elsted. Nothing really gets discussed or decided, because it has all been discussed and decided decades ago by tradition, and certainly not consciously by us. We will play most of the opponents we played last year. We will struggle to fill the first couple of games. We will do nets, twice, in early May. We will charge £50 for a membership that allows a season of no match fees thereafter, and £75 to include children as well. We will float the idea of a foreign tour and then abandon it for another season. We will buy 2 bats, a box of balls and a set of batting gloves. Someone will suggest that someone else writes a book about the Club.

Then Spring trips in slowly behind. You notice one day when you walk the dog, that there are snowdrops where there weren't snowdrops the day before. Everything is in motion with new life. Tiny vermilion leaves appear on the huge trees in the park opposite, and the rooks are every-where, carrying bunches of twigs to make their nests. There is a palpable sense of something drawing close. A fixture list is drafted out and circulated around the regulars. A summary of the previous season does the rounds, if anyone has the energy to produce it. Names that you haven't heard for six months ripple expectantly across your lips: Cheriton, East Meon, Goodwood, Adlestrop, Kings Somborne, Hawkesbury Upton. The newspaper runs an article foreshadowing the coming County Cricket season, and you feel it all bearing down on you like an express train.

One Sunday evening you bring the old Slazenger bag down from its top shelf and start to check it out. It is a futile exercise, as everything that you left in it when you put it away in September is still there, slightly more dog-eared and slightly less fit for purpose, in March. Just like you, in fact.

Love is in the air, so sometimes this is when you take your wallet for a private visit to the local sports shop, in the age old belief that new kit will make a difference. It won't. The dopamine neurotransmitter goes into overdrive and, before you know it, you have a pile of expensive new kit lined up on the counter. But dopamine is about the hunt, not the having, and by the time you have reached home again the chemical high has been replaced by the quiet and regretful knowledge that new kit of itself won't change anything.

Then you come to an evening net, and there they all are, the cast of this gentle sit-com. The Land Agent is as loud as he was the previous summer, and The Accountant still removes your middle stump with the first ball he bowls. The Major, it turns out, has wintered well and has regained two of the four stone he lost a year ago, much to the relief of those who treasure him for his Falstaff-like role in the team. The Breeder is in New Zealand selling cattle sperm, and why not? He sends a text message from the balmy Auckland sunshine saying without a shred of irony that he wishes he could be there, wishes he could share with us the Hampshire drizzle. The Farmer is there with his son, who teams up with mine to pour laconic scorn on the increasingly pathetic efforts of their fathers. The IT man is there, doomed forever to be trying something new to make it all happen. The Investor is there, beaming away and sending down juicy leg stump half volleys just like he did in the old days. The Grenadier is there, immaculate in his whites, and bowling mortar bombs. The long wait is nearly over for us. Another season is nearly on us.

But then of course there is more to it all than expectation.

Perhaps our cricket also provides us with a tiny window onto a world that is disappearing as fast as grains of sand run through cupped hands.

Our cricket gives us laughter. Even the direst of matches, the most forlorn pitches, and the grimmest oppositions make us smile. We laugh equally at each other's successes and failures. Most often we laugh at ourselves collectively, and, as we do so, we marvel at the sequence of tiny genetic miracles that threw us all together in the first place, and then gave us enough fun to keep it going long, long after its best-before date.

It gives us space, when so many things in life crowd in on us. Space to move around freely, and to watch time drift past without feeling guilt for it. Space not to feel bad about the absence of deadlines. A match allows a rare opportunity to be nothing more than a harmless part of someone else's view. Sometimes, there needs to be space in life for doing next to nothing, and cricket provides it.

Our cricket also provides us with a shameless piece of occasional escapism from this age of the information superhighway, the 24-hour convenience store and the endless subliminal messaging of the marketing men. It drags us away from the tyranny of the waiting e-mail, and the guilt of the 'calls missed' register on the mobile phone. To field idly at long-off in the evening sunshine is to peep back over the wall to when things moved slower, cost less and didn't always need to signify something. At a time of digital abundance, the whole glorious point of cricket is that so much of it is utterly pointless.

The White Hunters, and clubs like it, represent pay-back time for all us non-gladiators, children whose schools gave up on our right to at least be taught the basics of these sports. Having never been allowed to play, by virtue of our relative incompetence, at a time when others around us played twice a week, we now play as often as we like. Meanwhile, many of the ones who scored endless schoolboy fifties in their youth and received endless new accolades at morning assembly, got bored of the whole deal, or became large and driven men elsewhere, never playing on into relaxed adulthood. And even though Thatcher and Blair between them sold off just about every playing field that wasn't nailed down by legal covenant, for which neither must ever be forgiven, it seems that the pipeline of new players is in pretty good shape.

Our own team's children who now turn out to play for us pretty regularly, are by and large far better than we would have been at their age. And bigger. And funnier. And freer. And lippier. And probably better adjusted. And the best thing of all is that we still don't need to be CRB checked to play cricket with them. Just.

So it gives us opportunity, when so many doors to sporting endeavour were slammed in our faces decades before. For some reason, adults in Britain seem to be expected to watch team sports, not play them, and it is a fine feeling still to be one of the chosen few heading off for a pre-match pint on a sunny Saturday lunchtime. Our 2012 fixture list shows us as playing 18 matches over the summer, which is probably 18 more than many cricket lovers play in any decade after they leave school.

I have lost count of the number of innocent social conversations that have led to someone new to our team heading up to his attic to retrieve an old Gunn and Moore bag that he long thought to have seen the last of, and rubbing oil on an old Hunts County bat that last got used three weeks after his finals. Cricket is like that. It just is.

And the joke is that you really can get better. In my late forties, and frustrated after a diabolical previous season, I dragged myself off to the indoor school at Hove to try and mend just a little bit of my grotesque batting technique. The ancient coach fired a bucket of balls at me out of the bowling machine, and then said that though he had identified twenty things I was doing wrong, he would concentrate on repairing just three. Thus I started the new season holding my bat out behind me like Graham Gooch did, jerking my head up during the bowler's delivery stride like Michael Vaughan used to do, and flexing my wrists like Sunil Gavaskar. It all probably looked pathetic to people who weren't themselves doing it, but something clicked. For once in my life, I didn't believe that I had to hit the next ball into kingdom come on the basis that it would almost certainly be my last; for a few glorious games, I even started pushing the thing into gaps, and running two or even three. My average tripled to 36 that year, before gently declining back to where it had once been. After all, mediocrity is a hard habit to break entirely.

In a relentless world of style over substance and image over just about everything, the White Hunters have managed to gather around them, both within the team and among the oppositions we love to play, a group of individuals entirely untroubled by either. There is something faintly comforting about being in the company of people who just get on with it. The first draft of this book had pencilled in a chapter on some of our internal disagreements, but there turned out to be so few that the idea had to be scrapped. And anyway, such that there had been, were our own private business.

In an age of screens, where the mainstream of human ingenuity seems to be directed at creating virtual – as opposed to real life- experiences, activities like White Hunter cricket come as a powerful antidote. After all, what could be less virtual than to stare behind yourself at three splattered stumps and a grinning wicket keeper? Afternoons spent among friends in a shared endeavour, be it ever so creaky and aimless, provide a tiny but important stretch of mental green-belt to the stresses and strains of everything else that goes on. Whatever your activity might be is not important, it is just life-enhancing to have one at all.

Halfway between some barking old Brigadier who is utterly resistant to change of any sort unless it is violently rightwards, and the hand-wringing, damp-eyed, resentful Islington apologist against all things British, lurks the reasonable 90% of the population. It is from these people that spring those who understand the beautiful irony of the game in all its facets. They accept that every good thing has to evolve to keep good, just as every precious thing must be protected from thoughtless alteration. To say that the game is peculiarly English is not some nationalist drumbeat, but a simple statement of belongingness. I cannot think of another country on earth where the White Hunter Cricket Club would have survived, and even thrived, without being ridiculed or banned.

Finally, at a time in which everything has to have meaning and context, our cricket most often has neither, match to match, season to season, decade to happy decade, the only point of it all is to provide a bit of fun and make ourselves happy. If the bi-product is to bring happiness and curiosity to others as well, then so much the better.

Five years ago, The Tree-Hugger and I sat down in The Harrow at Steep, and found ourselves trying to work out, not for the first time, what it was that had enabled the club to totter on into its third decade. The conversation quickly moved on to something less existential and … bingo … there was the answer! The club has survived precisely because no one can be bothered for long enough to work out the reason why. There has been precious little self-analysis and even less agonising about the subject. And absolutely no blazers. Each season it just seems that the same group of people rather fancy dressing up in off-white and playing this bemusing game together. Such lack of psychological complexity would leave Carl Jung simultaneously lost for words and clients.

Cricket is far too important to be left to the ECB, the MCC or any other set of initials, come to that. When the wreckers like 'Sir' Allen Stanford came on the scene for thirty pieces of silver a few years back, cricket just shrugged its shoulders and knew that he would eventually disappear, leaving life to go on as normal. Cricket, like they keep reminding us on Test Match Special, is bigger than any individual who plays it, even though some of our larger members could probably give it a run for its money.

Just as all is well with the world when brilliant teams dominate test matches and 20/20 tournaments, so it is when teams like The Hammer Bottom Butsers, The Bohemians, The Codrington Cobblers, The Rennergades, The Rainmen and The White Hunters prop up the other end of the quality pyramid. And just as the sport needs its Muralitharans and Gayles, so it needs its Yacht Designers and Grenadiers. The way we look at it, we unselfishly allow other stars to shine more brightly around us. Without people like us doing what we do each summer, a layer of more skilful cricketers would have to blink into the spotlight of mediocrity.

It is one thing for us all to have been part of a club that has cheerfully plumbed the trenches of under-achievement for 25 years, but it will be another thing altogether to know when to pull the curtain down on it for good. Some say that it should be allowed to pass to the next generation, and not one of us would object in principal if they really wanted it, save to wonder how we had produced children with such a lack of ambition. Another view is that it should continue till we are all heading for, or well into our sixties. However, we used to play such a team long ago, and we watched it going from Corinthian to crocked in the flash of an eye, by which time it was far too late for them to restore the charm and dignity that had once been an essential part of their character.

For myself, I tend towards the supernova theory, where the club simply compresses itself into a black hole at the stroke of midnight on a particular named day. I have a vision of final match of the final tour coming to an end with a tense one-wicket victory over the Kandahar Occasionals in the red Afghan dirt. And there, walking back to the pavilion with his bat held high by way of acknowledgement of the crowd's applause for his chanceless half century, comes the man of the match in the much-evolved shape of The Human Sieve.

Then the players fade off into the distance. They leave only the team's kit bag behind them, getting smaller and smaller and smaller until all that remains of their existence is a left-handed batting glove with the name 'Mason' taped on to it, with the disembodied voices of Jonathan Agnew and Victor Marks burbling comfortingly off into the ether beyond.

APPENDICES

Appendix 1

Club Records 1986-2011

Played :	277
Won :	111
Lost :	131
Drawn :	22
Tied :	3
Abandoned :	5
Disputed :	2
Called off due to Tragedy:	1
Opposition failed to turn up :	2

Highest Total by the White Hunters:
281-6 vs Jungle Bunnies
at Brockwood, 1990

Highest Total against the White Hunters:
295-8 by Rorkes'Drifters
at Winchester 2004

Lowest Total by White Hunters:
32 vs King Alfred's College
at Bar End, Winchester 1987

Lowest Total against White Hunters:
58 by Goudhurst,
at Goudhurst, Kent 1997

Biggest victories
By 165 runs vs Jungle Bunnies
at Brockwood 1990
By 9 wickets vs Relics and Rascals, Brockwood 2004
By 9 wickets vs Scottsmen
at Chedworth, 1992
By 8 wickets vs Broadhalfpenny Brigands,
Hambledon 2000
By 8 wickets vs Codrington Cobblers, 1998

Biggest defeats
By 172 runs vs Tillington
at Tillington 1996
By 9 wickets vs Ebernoe
at Ebernoe 2010
By 8 wickets vs Rennergades
at Fontmell Magna 2001
By 8 wickets vs Codrington Cobblers, Brockwood 1999
By 8 wickets vs Goodwood Estate
at Goodwood 1995

Partnerships
1st 159 vs Kitchin Cabinet
at Churchers College 2010
2nd 119 vs Ovington
at Brockwood 1996
3rd 158 vs Major's Minors at Cound, Shropshire 1995
4th 87 vs Plums
at Brockwood 1997

5th 166 vs Rhinos
at Brockwood 1990
6th 128 vs Rhinos
at Winchester College 2003
7th 109 vs Rainmen
at Brockwood 2011
8th 60 vs Kitchin Cabinet
at Winchester College 1999
9th 69 vs Bohemians
at Winchester College 1997
10th 46 vs All Whites
at Winchester College 1993

Hundreds (4)

102* The Timber Matting Contactor,
vs Major's Minors, Cound 1995
101* The Accountant vs Major's Minors, Cound 1995
101* The Farmer vs Codrington Cobblers
at Adlestrop 2002
100* The Cricketer vs Black Hearts
at Brockwood 1995

Fifties

About 82 at the last count, of which The Farmer has 10

Bowling:

Best
7-4-9-5 The Brand Manager vs Goudhurst,
at Goudhurst, Kent 1997

11-3-14-5 The Accountant vs Codrington Cobblers
at Adlestrop 1996
5-1-21-5 The Yacht Designer vs East Meon
at East Meon 2006
4-0-28-5 The Garden Statue vs Cheriton
 at Brockwood 2000
3-1-5-4 The Land Agent vs West Meon
at West Meon 2002
0.3-0-0-3 The Author, vs Jungle Bunnies
at Brockwood 1993
11-5-12-1 The Timber Matting Contractor vs Tillington
at Tillington 1988

Worst
1-0-25-0 The Author vs Cheriton
at Brockwood 1994

Hat Tricks
The Author vs The Jungle Bunnies
at Brockwood 1993
The Tree Seller vs Ovington Overs
at Brockwood 1993
The Tree Hugger vs Rennergades
at Fontmell Magna 1995

Appendix 2

List of Oppositions (73) in chronological order

1. Rhinos
2. Easton Royal All-Stars
3. Owslebury Occasionals
4. Tillington CC
5. Widcombe Wanderers
6. King Edward VII Hospital Midhurst
7. Goodwood Metalcraft
8. Appletreewick CC
9. Bolton Abbey CC
10. Austin and Wyatt
11. Jungle Bunnies
12. Marlingford CC
13. Goodistone CC
14. Little Durnford CC
15. Cheriton CC
16. Nationwide BS
17. Poltimore Arms CC
18. Bridgtown CC
19. Black Hearts
20. Scottsmen
21. Common Lawyers
22. James Harris Estate Agents
23. Ovington Overs
24. Goodwood Estate CC
25. All Whites

26. Stranded Whales
27. Bohemians
28. Rennergades
29. Codrington Cobblers
30. Kitchin Cabinet
31. Shropshire Strugglers
32. Major's Minors
33. Itchen Stoke CC
34. Cotswold Lions
35. Clapham Casuals
36. Alresford CC
37. Plums CC
38. Gardening Club
39. Goudhurst CC
40. Folly's Farm Old Spots
41. Georgian Group
42. HMS Collingwood
43. Greenhill Growlers
44. Vagabonds
45. Catchiteers
46. Tusmore Park
47. Dorton Dynamos
48. White and Bowker
49. Broadhalfpenny Down Brigands
50. Saumur CC
51. A Team of Frenchmen
52. The Mercers Company
53. The Unknowns
54. Hammer Bottom Butsers

55. West Meon CC
56. Naturetrek
57. Rorkes' Drifters
58. Fantasians
59. Relics and Rascals
60. East Meon CC
61. Winchester College Staff
62. Prodigals
63. Kings Somborne
64. Elstead CC
65. Easton Gentlemen
66. Poynings CC
67. Ebernoe CC
68. Hawkesbury Gentlemen
69. Armagnac Bigorre CC
70. Toulouse CC
71. Rainmen
72. Winchester Doctors
73. Stowe School Staff

Appendix 3

List of Grounds (63)

Avon
Chewton Mendip

Berkshire
East Woodhay

Buckinghamshire
Ashfold School,
Stowe School

Devon
Poltimore

Dorset
Ashmore,
Fontmell Magna,
Iwerne Minster,
Powerstock

France
Armagnac-Bigorre,
Saumur,
A Field North of Saumur

Gloucestershire
Adlestrop,
Chedworth,
Hawkesbury Upton
RAC Cirencester

Hampshire
Alresford Park,
Broadhalfpenny Down,
Brockwood Park,
Cheriton,
Churchers College,
Chute,
East Meon,
Easton,
Hawkley,
HMS Collingwood,
Hurstbourne Priors,
King Alfred College,
Kings Somborne,
Lord Wandsworth College,
Petersfield,
St Cross,
West Meon,
Winchester College, Kingsgate,
Winchester College, Meads

Kent
Goudhurst,

Kilndown

London
Emmanuel School,
St Pauls School Hammersmith

Norfolk
Goodistone,
Marlingford

Oxfordshire
Merton College, Oxford,
Tusmore Park

Somerset
Bridgetown

Shropshire
Shrewsbury School,
Cound

Surrey
Elstead

West Sussex
Cowfold,
Ebernoe,
Elsted,
Folly Farm,

Chiddingfold
Goodwood,
King Edward VII Hospital, Midhurst
Lurgashall,
Tillington

Wiltshire
Burbage,
Fonthill,
Great Durnford,
Shalbourne

Yorkshire
Appletreewick,
Bolton Abbey